A LOVE SONG

The evolution of human consciousness

LILY BAILEY

BALBOA.
PRESS

A DIVISION OF HAY HOUSE

ISBN: 978-1-4525-4357-4 (sc)
ISBN: 978-1-4525-4358-1 (e)

Balboa Press books may be ordered through booksellers or by contacting:

Balboa Press
A Division of Hay House
1663 Liberty Drive
Bloomington, IN 47403
www.balboapress.com
1-(877) 407-4847

Printed in the United States of America
Balboa Press rev. date: 1/18/2012

PREFACE

Before you begin reading, let me clarify a few terms and ideas in the book:

My fundamental understanding of God has changed tremendously since I was a child sitting in a Methodist church. I still see God as love – they are one and the same, inseparable. I also still see God as the creator of all that is, although I now see his creation as being *only* love. God is the originating consciousness. He is the ultimate truth who extended his love to us so that we might learn to know ourselves. Love and judgment cannot coexist. God is only love.

When I began reading spiritual books, I found myself often confused by their use of the term, ego. The ego I speak of is not Freud's ego. It resembles Freud's model only in that it represents a division in our mind. The spiritual ego is a nonexistent entity that we mistake as ourselves. It is a habit of mind – in a mind that is in the habit of avoidance. It is itself a defense mechanism. Thus, whereas Freud might conceive of a healthy ego, from a spiritual point of view, this is impossible.

IN THE GARDEN

Before there was time, we were one, a steady stream of consciousness, without beginning, without end, an energy field of love's awareness. We lived in a state of continual abundance, we did not know loss, we could not imagine deprivation. We could not imagine separation. We were one with the eternal consciousness, we were one with God. There was only love, the energy of the universe entire. Our love gave us peace, deep and abiding. Our love gave us joy overflowing. In peace we rested in our being. In joy we sought to extend ourselves, to give of our love, for that is love's nature. The eternal consciousness, God, extended himself in his love, to create new awareness, these were as his children, from them he withheld nothing. In full awareness they were one. They loved as their father loved. They too sought to extend their love, to create from their abundance, to give of themselves to their father whom they loved.

It was as a beautiful chorus, delicate interweaving harmonies, Baritones, bass, sopranos in perfect pitch, each contributing to the beauty of the whole. One without the other would know no balance; the beauty would be lessened without all. And then perhaps one voice raised itself ever so slightly above the others. Awareness shifted its focus. It looked away from God, if only for an instant. In that moment, God's children realized they could look away from their father, he had given them free will; they were not prisoners of his love. Separate voices could now be heard, singing to their father, singing of love but not with the rest. If one could sing above another, perhaps God could love greater. In that instant God's children believed in loss. The harmony began to falter, notes became discordant. God's children began to believe in difference, separation, preference. The harmonies fell, as did his children, from perfect grace.

Those who had known only love now perceived its loss, they came to believe that which was not so. The void left in the absence of love became shame, profound and shattering. It was unbearable. They began to hide from each other and from themselves. They sought to escape the terrible burden of being without love. Pain drove them further from their home. They became lost souls who knew not even self. In their confusion they came to believe that their father was the source of their suffering. That he had cast them out for their imperfections and deemed them unworthy of his love. They believed themselves exiles from the garden, never realizing that it had been their choice to go.

Perhaps we drifted for a while, awareness knowing only shame. Perhaps as his children departed, God called them to return, but allowed them to go, as was their choice. The farther away, the louder the call, but we could no longer hear. God who knows nothing of shame could no longer speak to us in way we would understand. And so, we settled in a new home, a place where we could find temporary solace. It would show us what we now believed to be true, while gently teaching us it was not so. We believe it is possible to exist in separation from our father and so ours is a world of separation. Instead of unity, here there are opposites and opposing forces. For day there is night, for black, white. We are male and female, divided even within our form. Within the play of opposites is life, it is the balance, it is the truth we seek. Our beautiful earth sits perfectly poised between sun and moon. The entirety of our physical existence held in this delicate balance. The sun shines, the rains come, the plants grow, we breathe the air they create for us, so we may learn division is not so. We see past separation, we return home knowing that truly we have never left. Our lessons can be as simple as a sunrise or a flowers bloom. Our planet holds life in abundance; it is a vibrant energy system. Life can only exist in God's love. If we allow it the earth can lead us back to our true home.

One can only see what one believes. The earth reflected our new beliefs while also holding truth. We however, have been largely unwilling to see love. In order to see truth we had to be willing to look through the lie of shame. That was not our intention. We had forgotten our true nature. We had come to believe that to look upon God's love was to face annihilation. We have used the earth to hide. We placed our focus here and found that if our focus was narrow enough we might no longer feel shame. And so our focus narrowed to a single point. As experience continued we came to believe that we were the point rather than the focus. That which was distraction was given self, the ego was born. Our true self became only an observer, pushed to the background, relegated to powerlessness. This we willingly accepted to escape the belief we were unworthy of love. Our true self remains, it is always here, for most of us it is simply unaware that it has been lulled to sleep, hypnotized by the antics of distraction.

In Truth, thought is the entirety of our being. Because we have narrowed our thought to a single point, we have locked our self in form. We have come to believe there is *only* form, each point separate from the other. So long as we hide from pain we imprison ourselves here. This is the original catch 22 and the root of everything that does not make sense in our world. **The ego came into existence to keep us from experiencing pain, yet it must maintain the pain to continue to exist.** This creates an inherent split in our psyche. We exist in this world on three levels. We are the ego, the focus, the part of us which experiences the world through perception and believes itself to be form. We are also the subconscious, the level of our mind in which we try to hide pain. Our "thoughts" may follow the ego, while our emotions follow the subconscious. Because the ego works to keep us from looking at the subconscious, we may have no understanding whatsoever of our emotions. In order to free ourselves, we must make the decision to place our focus on this level of consciousness. We must face our personal truth in order to embrace universal Truth. These two levels of mind are only illusion, our true self, the observer waits only for us to remember this is so.

When we begin to move past the ego's dominion, we start our spiritual journey. We move into the emotional part of our being which is the subconscious. The subconscious is a continuum of expanding awareness. It begins with the point where emotion sits next to and goes hand in hand with the ego. In order to move past this point you must be willing to examine and begin to relinquish the false ideas you acquired about yourself in this lifetime. Whatever painful events you began storing in this space as a child act as a barrier to Truth. The more you hide from them, the stronger their hold. The farther you move away from ego, the stronger the pull of your own spirit. The events of our life are not random. We are not at the mercy of fate or a vengeful god. The part of us which remains connected to Truth knows that we must return home. It seeks the reintegration of our mind's awareness, to end the division between ego, subconscious and spirit, so that our mind can be one. When our mind is one, so are we one with God.

Life is the journey home to our source. It is the movement from a narrow point of focus to all-encompassing awareness, from self-imposed illusion to Truth. You are not alone on this journey. The events of your life are carefully orchestrated to teach the lessons you must learn. Our spirit, which remains one with all life, sets for us a path in each life. One that will lead us home should we choose to follow it. It can still hear the voice of God. He continues to call to us, we have only to listen.

Part I-

THE EGO

Chapter 1

THE EGO IS BORN

The voice in your head is not you. This should come as a great relief.

The ego is nothing, we think it is everything. It is the voice in your head that attempts to fill every second of your being, leaving us no space for true thought, just endless gibberish. It is the "monkey mind" swinging through the branches from tree to tree, random thought to random worry. It is forever in need of something, it is never at peace. It can create strife out of nothing. It will happily argue with imaginary people over imaginary issues. This is the ego: It does not make sense, it just makes trouble.

The world you experience through perception is an illusion. The ego can *only* see through perception. This is a very old idea, dating back to the time of the earliest Indian civilizations. Hindus, Buddhist and many others accept this premise as fact. The reason you experience this illusion is that you hold false beliefs about yourself. You believe that you are deeply flawed and thus you experience a world that proves this is so. You believe that it is possible to separate yourself from your creator thus you see a world of opposing forces. You believe you have lost your connection to God and thus you experience a world that can give you only loss. Here there is only impermanence. That which you hold today, is gone tomorrow. As we have divided ourselves from God, so have we divided our mind. The divided mind is the mechanism of division from God. Everything we experience in this world seeks to teach us this is so. God calls to us always. Integrating the divisions in our mind will reestablish our true selves and we will be able to "go" home. To do this we must be willing to face Truth. We must examine our own thought processes and be willing to give up that which does not make sense. We must surrender all, which is not truth. We must recognize the ego for what it is, or more accurately for what it is not. It is not you.

We come into this world believing in loss. If we did not believe this we would not be able to experience it. This creates within us a divided mind. At birth we exist at two levels. We are spirit which holds truth and subconscious where we hold shame, the spirit knows only joy and the subconscious only loss. Thus, as infants we live in a state of balance and imbalance determined solely by emotional experience. We are warm, dry, our bellies full, all is well. We are cold, wet, hungry, we are without what is needed to be well. We exist either in joy or deprivation. The infant's brain has yet to develop so that it can experience itself as a separate entity. It exists as awareness, an integrated part of its surroundings.

All babies are not the same. They are born with different

temperaments, or different tolerance for imbalance. This is a spiritual issue. We bring into each life the mistaken ideas we held onto from the last life. The more mistakes we hold onto the less tolerance we have for imbalance, this is the child's nature. However, balance at this point in life is largely an external issue. The child's level of spiritual development interacts with its current environment, which may or may not encourage balance. It is nature vs. nurture. In time a balance will be struck between the two and the child's identity established.

As the baby grows, its brain develops and it begins to experience the world in a different way. It starts to recognize itself as a distinct entity, separate from its surroundings. It develops the ability to focus its awareness. It masters what is called object permanence, the understanding that just because you can no longer see something does not mean it no longer exists. It is now possible to want what you do not have. What before was simple imbalance is now need. Rather than focusing on permanence, the child focuses on loss. It develops a distinct set of preferences for the way its external world should be ordered. It ties the presence or absence of things to its emotional state of being. If mother is here all is well, if mother is not here there is pain. It does not like to experience pain. In order to communicate preference and restore satisfactory order to its world, it begins to develop language. A third level of mind is coming into being, the ego. The ego believes it can manipulate and control the external world and by so doing, avoid pain. As we develop focus our experience of pain changes. We become aware that it is something which exists inside of our self. We believe that if we focus on things outside of our self we can avoid the pain.

The ego, then, is a decision made in our early childhood to externalize self in order to avoid suffering. It is a placing of our focus on what is outside of ourselves and looking to it to bring us happiness and love. It is a decision which makes suffering inevitable as love can only be experienced within. It is the ever so human desire to avoid pain rather than deal with it. This is a child's coping mechanism, hands on ears, eyes closed, humming a repetitive tune, the belief that pain can be ignored and thus not experienced. In our desire to avoid pain, we instead, store it in the subconscious layer of our mind where the ego can later draw upon it in order to strengthen itself. It will act as a barrier between self and spirit. Before the subconscious is fully formed, a child experiences the world mainly through the ego or through the spirit. They have a tendency to exist in joy, fully in the moment; this is because the child can still experience the world from pure spirit. Here is the child that poets and philosophers exhort us to be like, the one that plays happily in the park without a care in the world. Yet, within this same child is the ego. You will encounter it when it is time to leave the park and the child who doesn't want to leave throws an award-winning temper tantrum for all to see. They have two distinct sides, these little ones.

For a child who is experiencing pure joy, to suddenly have the external source of it removed is excruciatingly painful. The ego tells them that joy is outside of them but it has not yet taught them to deflect the pain of its loss. These first cuts are indeed the deepest and the severity of them will help to determine how firmly the ego will take control. Someone who experiences a traumatic childhood will have to develop strong defense mechanisms. That is essentially what the ego is. Almost all children will experience the withdrawal of their caregivers love. At time in our physical development, when emotion is our only way of knowing, we find that it is possible to lose the one thing we need the most. Even in the best of circumstances, a parent will, at least for a short time, withdraw unconditional love from their child. It is simply the nature of our physical being. A sleep- deprived parent will feel displeasure towards their child when woken up for the fifth time in one night. A child will feel the loss of this love, he will experience it as a diminishment of self or shame. It is a replay or our original error with our true creator. Just as a true parent loves a child always, so too does God love us always, but we do not believe this to be true.

A human being who has not experienced enlightenment is incapable of perfect love. Such people tend to live on mountain tops and be celibate. Thus, this pattern is inevitable at this time. The degree to which a child internalizes shame depends on several factors, the evolutionary state of the child's soul and the degree to which the parent initially and continually withdraws love; nature and nurture.

We come to believe, at a very early age, at an emotional level which is our true self, that we are undeserving of perfect love. Being incapable of receiving it, we are thus incapable of giving it, and the cycle continues. The original loss then, is that of our true self. It is this, and only this, that separates us from God. Having lost this sense of self, we spend the rest of our lives looking for it. Most of us spend lifetime after lifetime looking in the wrong place. The reason for this is our ego.

You might think of the ego in this way. Imagine that you are very upset about something that has happened, something that you feel responsible for and that you believe has caused great and irreparable harm to yourself and others. You can hardly stand yourself, the pain is virtually intolerable. You turn on the television, you don't even care what you watch, you simply must have something else to focus on other than the pain of being you. You start watching and just keep watching, the more you watch the better you are able to ignore your feelings. You are afraid to stop watching because you might start to focus again on the pain you are certain will destroy you. You watch and watch and watch. You come to prefer the TV over anything else, regardless of what show is on. You watch so long you come to identify yourself with the television. After a long enough time you come to believe the TV *is* you. You may know you have other feelings and emotions but it is just so much easier to keep watching. You believe that to give up the television would be to give up a part of yourself.

Somewhere around the age of twelve basic personality has been set. The lessons that will need to be dealt with in this life established. The ego has become what, if unexamined, it will be for the rest of one's life. It has looked outside of itself and decided that what it sees is what it will forever regard as normal. Around this idea of normalcy it will create a series of habitual thoughts. These thought patterns are established at a very young age, mainly by the people closest to the child. There will be negative and positive patterns, sometimes far more of one than another. They are like endless repeating loops of thought. The ego will have created its labels, or word choices it will apply to objects. It will know what it likes and what it does not and to what extent it feels it must share these likes and dislikes with others. It will have labeled certain human beings as acceptable and others as not. It will have decided how close another's thought patterns must be to its own to be worthy of attention. It will have decided what set of circumstances allow one to feel OK. Under what external circumstances one might briefly be happy and when one must be unhappy. The ego will be far more comfortable and secure in situations of stress. From here on the ego will gauge everything according to what it has already set as acceptable. All events will be measured according to past events and thus not truly experienced. The level of the subconscious may be quite full leaving it extremely difficult to have any meaningful connection to spirit.

The ego comes into being as the child begins to develop language. They will essentially be one and the same. Language acts as a barrier to true experience. If you watch a beautiful sunset and sit in peaceful silence, your breath stilled, then you experience the sunset from your true emotional center or spirit. On the other hand, if you watch the sunset and you think that it is "beautiful, that the colors are really pretty, they are pink and orange like a creamsicle. It is really getting late but I hate to miss this. Too bad my friend/boyfriend/girlfriend is not here to share it with me. They would really enjoy it even though I am mad at them for what they did last week. What is that color? I don't think I have ever seen it before. I don't have any clean clothes to wear tomorrow. Wow, I can't believe what George wore to work today; he must be losing it. How could he get that promotion instead of me?"

The ego is at the heart of the "terrible twos." Its favorite words are "I" and "mine". It is ever wanting. We accept this as a normal step in human development. We believe it is necessary to exist as a separate entity in order to grow. This is not necessarily so but it is the path we have chosen to take. Prior to language an infant's "thoughts" are emotion rather than verbal. They are of love or its loss. Infants who are denied love will fail to thrive just as if they had been denied nutrition.

Once the ego has done its work, our connection to spirit tends to be blocked by the contents of our subconscious, or our false beliefs. From the age of 12 to 30, or so, we tend to operate on the level of the ego and the subconscious. The ego operates through linguistic thought, subconscious through emotion. This is why it is quite possible for your head to tell you one thing, and your heart to tell you another. You are literally of divided mind. The ego however, if it has done its job well in childhood, has quite a stockpile of negative emotions to draw upon. In fact when it has no other thought pattern to draw on (it's bored) it will likely just dredge up some particularly depressing pattern that has absolutely nothing to do with your present circumstances, anything to avoid a quiet mind. There is nothing more dangerous to the ego than a quiet mind. It will just focus on the depressing pattern, which will likely bring up other depressing patterns and then, you are...depressed.

If the ego has done its job particularly well, the individual will have a narrow range of emotions. The ego operates at the level of fear. If it can, through its repetitive loops, convince you that everything you have in the subconscious is terrifying than you will be more than happy to let the ego reign supreme. You will cover fear with anger. This is quite complementary to the ego's mission. So long as you are angry at others you will have no time to take an honest look at yourself. This is a quality frequently found in teens and young adults. Whatever has gone wrong is someone else's fault, usually their mothers. Fortunately, most of those grow out of this, at least to some extent. We begin taking more responsibility for ourselves. As we get closer to middle age, we begin to feel more comfortable in ourselves. We might begin to recognize that some of these thoughts that go through our mind don't really make much sense and are in fact harmful. Perhaps we decide to stand in front of the mirror daily and tell ourselves how great we are. We have had many new experiences which did not jive with the ego's labels. We might give some of them up, or at least alter them a bit. Somewhere along the way we develop the ability of self-reflection.

As we enter middle age, most of us have figured out we are not the center of the universe. We have given up at least the most glaring errors we held about ourselves. Some space has been cleared in the subconscious and we may again be able to glimpse our true spirit. There may be more times when the voice in our head is not that of the ego, but that of our soul. You may begin to recognize Truth. You know Truth by the way it feels. There is a feeling that goes with certainty. It is quiet, still and deeply comforting. When you have found this feeling, you have found Truth. We feel that we know ourselves better now than ever before. We like ourselves.

As we experience truth, we internalize it. We make it a part of ourselves. Every label you remove and Truth you internalize narrows the ego's dominion. No longer can it run the old thoughts, when you know they are not true. It may still try at times, but you will "give it no mind." You will not focus your mind upon what you know is untrue, thus the ego's ability to interpret the world through its unique perception lessons. You begin to share more of the world with others.

If all has gone well, which it sometimes may, by the time we are old, we have learned great Truth. Our attachment to our body has been broken by our attachment to our spirit. The level of subconscious is nearly empty. The ego may still speak, but we do not listen...we know. We return to the place where we began in this life. We listen to our feelings, not the rambling voice. We seek balance. We place value on love, not on material items. All that is left is to remove the bucket itself. We must give up the original idea, which seemed to divide that which can only be one. We will all reach this place. We will all be called to give up that which is false for truth. When the time comes we will lay down this burden we have chosen to carry and be as we are, light, love the joy of creation, abiding peace, complete.

We will all reach this place...one day. We need not be old, it can happen any time we choose. This pattern of spiritual growth is very general, it certainly does not hold true for all. Spiritual enlightenment can come to the very young. I have heard stories of some like this; I have never met them. Lifetimes can be spent without much outward sign of spiritual advancement. I have met many like this.

Sometimes the ego does not weaken with age. For some, it dominates the entire life. It succeeds in holding spirit hostage to fear. It marshals anger to deal with every unfair situation. Life, it will see as unfair. If you believe the voice in your head is you, you may never stop to question it. If you hope to break its hold, you must recognize it for what it is, or more importantly, what it is not.

The mind, in this illusionary plane is divided into three parts; it is this division which creates and sustains our separation from God. We are a part of God, we are God, and we *must* separate ourselves in order to separate from him. The deepest part of us is Truth. It is our eternal self, a place where mind blends into pure consciousness. Here we may focus our consciousness and be as a drop, or release ourselves and be as the ocean. This is true consciousness or spirit. Here we hold no divisions. We know all, and all knows us. There is nothing here to hide. When we chose to believe in untruth, we created a division in our focused consciousness. We created an illusionary separate state. Our subconscious is the emotional part of our being. It can know both truth and can hold the false ideas we cling to about self. We can experience feelings of great joy or feelings of deep sorrow, depending on our willingness to accept Truth. As human beings we seek to avoid pain. Living without God's love is painful. In order to escape this painful state of being, we placed our focus away from the pain, thus creating a third level of mind, the ego. The ego is a defense mechanism, a distraction from that which we do not wish to experience. It comes into existence in the human mind when we begin to use language. Language itself serves as an intervening level between our true selves and experience. Rather than experience the moment as it is, we reinterpret it linguistically, thru the habituated "thought" of the ego.

The purpose of our lives is to reintegrate our mind, to become what we truly are. To do this one must recognize the ego for what it is, or more accurately is not. It is not you. Unless you have already made this realization, (and I believe it is quite possible to do this and be unaware of it) the voice that speaks in your head, rarely speaks for you. You will have times of deeper insight but you may or may not recognize them as Truth. You may or may not hold on to them and make them a part of your being. As we grow and mature, the pull of the ego should diminish, we should recognize greater truths. We should begin to know ourselves and our true spirit, this is if all goes well. As we all know, often times, it does not.

Chapter Two

EGOIC IDENTITY

The ego has no true identity. Because it is not real it cannot know itself, thus it lives in a constant state of fear. It is afraid that we might discover truth and no longer believe its lies. We have allowed it to capture our focus for far too long. We are all too accustomed to its noise. We do not know how to be without it. If, by some good fortune, we happen upon a moment of stillness…that moment is remembered. We may not even know why. For just an instant there was peace. Beneath the ego's chatter there is always peace. The ego knows this and seeks to make sure its chatter is constant so that you will never make this discovery.

Because the ego has no identity, it seeks to know itself through others. It looks to the world to tell it who it is. In its infancy, caregivers will do this. They will tell it that it is a boy or a girl, they will give it dolls or trucks or maybe both. By this choice of toys and clothing and watching its caregivers, the ego will come to understand what it means to be male or female. The caregivers will tell it if it is good or if it is bad, smart or unintelligent, capable of taking care of itself or not. They may tell it why, or they may not, it does not matter, the ego does not require reason. The ego will be especially adept at remembering the bad. The ego will decide, based upon what it is told in its childhood, what its relative position is to others. It must find a way to be special. If it has academic success it will decide it must be smarter than others. If it is told that it is beautiful, it will decide that it must be more attractive than others. If it cannot find an arena in which it has been praised, it will decide it must be worse than all the others. It will find its niche and it will always be in comparison to others and based on what others have told it about itself. The ego will look at the world it sees in its childhood and decide that this is the world as it should be. If there is peace in the home, than that is the way a home should be. If there is anger, abuse, neglect, than that is the way a home should be. It will decide what normal is, and this will be its reference for the rest of its life. The ego will seek to keep you in an environment in which it feels comfortable. So long as the ego dominates your thought processes it is virtually impossible to make significant changes in your way of life.

We create habits of egoic thought as we develop language. They frequently sound much like the words we hear our parents speak. We are told we can't do anything right and we begin to hear in our head… I can't do anything right. Certain patterns become tied to certain emotional responses. These patterns will grow as we do, until we reach the point that our basic identity is established. These thought loops will then repeat for the rest of one's life anytime the emotional trigger is present. When we feel the pain of having made a mistake we will say to our self, I can't do anything right. The ego will go to college parties, work Christmas parties, retirement parties and place itself in its accustomed world. It will run the thought loop it created long ago, I am the one no one wants to talk to. Or, conversely, I am the life of the party. It will find the place in the room that most suits its view of self. So long as this pattern goes unrecognized, it will continue. There is no space between the emotional response and the ego's litany that allows for self-reflection. If we remain in the ego's grasp we will never grow beyond the emotional responses we had as children.

The ego can only see itself through others eyes. The ego will spend its entire life measuring itself by others. It will determine its current worth according to how well those around it are doing. The body will be evaluated according to social standards. Is it too fat, or too thin? Are muscles large enough, nose small enough. Does it have more money than the neighbors, or other family members? Has it acquired more gadgets than its "friends?" To what extent is it living in deprivation? The ego lives always in deprivation. It will never have enough to feel secure because it is not possible for the ego to feel that way. It will thus attempt to acquire security through external means. It will make friends that reflect well upon it or it will make friends that reflect its view of normalcy. Either way, it will, for a moment feel secure. It will marry according to these parameters as well. It will acquire belongings it believes add to its security.

Because the ego needs to be better than others, it will be extremely critical. It has no choice but to bring other people down in order to boost itself up. The girl who identifies herself as the pretty one will not want to have friends who are prettier than she. She must be the prettiest to maintain her identity. She will be extremely critical of all women she believes might be attractive enough to be a threat to her. The same is true for intelligence. Those who identify themselves as smart will prefer to have friends who are decidedly less so. They do not want friends who are stupid, because that would reflect badly on them, just ones they have a distinct advantage over. One who identifies herself as the pretty girl may also believe she is not very intelligent and so she is a perfect match for the smart one.

In whatever way the ego has defined itself it must defend. Its only means of doing this is to convince itself of its brand of truth. A man who identifies himself as the one who understands the world and how it works will be extremely critical of any opposing view. The ego defends itself by degrading others. Its greatest threat is someone who identifies themselves in the same way. If it must be the best at something, then no one else can come close to challenging that point of view. The ego's identity is a house of cards, it is built on falsehood. Deep down it knows that out there somewhere there is someone whose skill is greater. If as a child the ego does not find its niche of superiority it will turn its criticism on its self. It is perfectly happy to do this. It is telling a slightly different version of the same lie. It may allow you to believe that you are the best at one thing but terrible at everything else. Regardless, criticism is its main tool of defense. If you are worse than everyone at everything this is a comfortable identity as far as the ego is concerned. With this definition the ego knows itself. That is all it is interested in.

The ego believes it is the roles it plays. It is a mother or father, son or daughter. It is a lawyer or cashier. This is how it defines itself to others, this is the relationship it holds with other. It knows the actions it is meant to take according to the role it is playing. Again it will have learned these roles by looking outside of itself. It will look to its own mother or father to determine how a parent should behave. It will expect its children to behave as they did. It will model its actions on what it has seen them do. If it cannot find satisfactory role models for human interactions it will find another way to define itself. It may decide to tie its identity completely to its profession. It will then look to co-workers, finding ones fitting its definition of normal and model its behavior after them.

In order to know how it compares to other, and thus know itself, it must carefully label everything and everyone. It must judge others so that it can judge itself. It must know what type of people it is superior to and what sort of people it is inferior to. It will create these labels so that they can be readily applied without thought. It must know what things are good and what things are not, so that it can judge quickly and assess its standing in any situation. The ego will not take time to examine the subtleties of a situation. The world to it is black and white, good or bad. It does not waste time considering others points of view. If others do not agree with them, they are of no value. If they are uneducated then those with a college degree have no common sense but still think they are better than everyone else. If they are educated than those who are not lack intelligence. The ego, if confronted with its own mistake, is quite content to lie to itself in order to preserve its point of view. It will believe its own lies. It will expect others to believe them as well.

Because the ego defines itself according to others it cannot ignore what it perceives as insult from others. It responds as if the words of others truly have the power to diminish it. No threat or challenge, however small, can go unanswered. It is constantly defending itself against those it believes define it. The ego is never to blame for any situation. It is incapable of taking responsibility for its actions. Whatever has gone wrong is in one way or another someone else's fault. The ego may go to great lengths to maintain this point of view. It is tremendously skilled at character assassination. It can find fault with anyone at any time and will claim that they knew it all along. Every problem in a relationship is because of the other person. This is the only belief it can hold. The world has told it who it is, thus the world is responsible for all events that act upon it. The ego will rage at God or fate or both. It can simultaneously blame unseen forces and those that are seen as well.

The ego rages at the world which created it. It knows itself to be powerless and so it insists on having power over others. Anger gives one a false sense of power. In one's experience of this emotion is the implication that you are superior to the person or situation which you believe is causing you to be angry. You could not be angry with someone if this were not so. You feel angry because someone has done something wrong. *You* have determined what is right, *you* have determined what is acceptable. The other person has not behaved according to your labels of right and wrong. You are justified in being angry. Because you feel angry, you do not feel weak. In fact, you can claim invulnerability. The other person's misbehavior is because of their weakness, not yours. The implication here is, of course, that others should behave according to your will. If they do not, you might have to accept that you do not order the universe or….you could just get really angry.

Anger is like fire, it destroys everything within its path. This is certainly quite evident in relationships. Love and anger do not exist in the same place. The problem with both anger and fire is that they destroy their source. For a time, a person experiencing anger will feel strong. They will yell, bully, torment or berate, but the body cannot sustain this behavior for very long. The person will be left exhausted and may actually go to sleep shortly after the rage has passed. People who experience anger on a regular basis have far more health problems than those who do not. Whereas a rage may leave a person noticeably spent, long term low level anger will slowly destroy its host. It is a cancer, if not cancer itself.

Anger is the most effective emotion to blocking spirit. The ego finds this a very effective method of self-preservation.

Below the anger is fear. The ego is always in a precarious position but it has a powerful ally. If it has done its job well the subconscious will be well stocked with pain and more than willing to follow the ego's direction. Emotion will be completely controlled by the ego. We allow the ego to paralyze us with fear, believing deep in our hearts that this is the way it must be. We are a species driven by fear. Fear of what we may lose, fear of what we may gain because we may then lose it. Fear insures that we will not look too deeply at self, and that we will never be happy for more than a short time. Fear lies behind every thought that something might go wrong. It is the source of all anxiety. We think it comes from the fragile condition we hold for a short time on this planet, in fact, it is fear of our true self. You are afraid you will make a mistake… you will. You are afraid something will go wrong with your plans…it will. You are afraid someone you love will die…they will. This is truth. If you were not afraid of the way YOU will deal with it, you would not be afraid. You are afraid of yourself.

According to the ego, we live on the edge of extinction. The world could end at any moment for any number of reasons. If you do not believe this, watch the nightly news: It is dominated by fear, as is virtually every other source of media we have in the United States. Nothing sells better than fear. We make movie after movie about the end of the world. There are asteroids about to collide with the earth, killer viruses, invading aliens and my personal favorite, giant killer bunnies. We are, and always have been, intent on scaring ourselves into a state of powerlessness. We believe that the earth is a place of scarcity, that there is not enough for all of us to survive. For our security we must hold on tightly to our possessions. We connect our physical safety to our acquisition of objects. The more we have the more secure we may tell our self we feel. Yet the more we have, the more we have to lose. Thus we must acquire more to reestablish our feeling of safety.

The ego knows our world is based on impermanence. There is nothing here that we can hold on to forever, so the ego spends its life attempting to control the uncontrollable. It believes it can find safety for itself and for its loved ones by carefully orchestrating their world. It assumes that if it is not ever vigilant that disaster will immediately strike. It must do things in a particular way to ensure the proper outcome. It insists that everyone around it behave as it sees fit. It may believe that if it follows a certain set of rules it will be safe. It may alternately believe that the rules do not apply to it and that it cannot suffer the consequences that others do because it is not like them.

The ego is a lie. It has no relationship to truth. It has all of the answers, all of the time. It never knows a moments questioning. It claims that it is the victim of its emotions when in fact emotions follow it completely. For a person living in the grip of the ego, there is no separation between thought and emotion. Ego leads the way and emotion follows. The ego will tell you that this is the only way it can be. The ego tells you that anger will protect you and that fear will keep you safe. It tells you that love is pain because you will lose it sooner or later. It tells you should not be happy because it will make it more painful when you become unhappy. It tells you that the best way to deal with pain is to ignore it, to refuse to feel it and suppress it deep inside you. It tells you that material goods will make you happy and that when that happiness wears off you should simply buy more. The ego will tell you *you* should be happy but it will never allow you to be. Never will it occur to the ego that it is nonsensical to look outside of one's self for something that is experienced within. In all things the ego is a contradiction.

We expect teenagers to be largely in the grip of the ego.

We also expect them to outgrow it. Unfortunately not everyone does. For many of us, even as teenagers, we are not completely dominated by ego. There are moments of clarity where truth may emerge. The older we get the more frequently we should experience this. For some of us however, the pain that is stored in our subconscious is of such an intense nature that it acts as a complete block to truth. It may leave a person completely cut off from their emotions, unable to experience the world as most people do. This is the state of the sociopath, psychopath, narcissist or personality disorder, in descending order of severity. They are the most resistant to modern day psychological methods of treatment because there is no room within their psyche for self-reflection. They cannot grow emotionally because the pain in their subconscious is too frightening to examine. They may be completely ego, with no connection to emotion. If there is a connection to emotion, it remains utterly in the control of the ego.

Chapter Three

PERCEPTION

The ego believes it is a body. The only way a body is capable of interacting with the world is through perception. It believes that what it sees, hears, smells, tastes and touches are the only things that are real. It lives in a world without mystery. What you see is what you get. It does not recognize that there may be different ways of processing the same information. As far as it is concerned if others do not reach the same conclusions based on the same input there is something wrong with the other person. There is only one way to view a situation...the ego's way.

Perception only becomes possible when a child develops the ability to focus. In the beginning it exists as if all sights and sounds are an integral part of the whole which they experience as one with themselves. As time goes on they begin to understand that sounds may be made by something that is distinctly not them. Things that they see are separate from them, distinct entities unto themselves. They need to make sense of these things. They begin to place labels on the things around them. Most caregivers are more than happy to help them do this. Likely at some point in their early development they will be bombarded by labels. The caregiver may point to herself and say "Mommy" and smile then make incredibly silly noises that make the baby laugh. The caregiver may slap the child in the face, knock it off its feet and scream "You better learn to call me Mommy." It is the same word, applied to the person who occupies the same position in the child's life, but does it have the same meaning? Attached to all of our labels are the emotional ideas we hold about them. The ego would tell you that this is not so, words are only words; they mean the same thing to everyone. Some words may be more emotionally charged than others. A blue lamp may be a device that provides light or it may be the instrument your brother used to crack you over the head when you were ten. A Tupperware washtub may be an old piece of junk or it may be the swimming pool where Barbie spent many a carefree summer day. Words can be very specific to an individual. Attached to many words are memories which may hold pleasure or pain. We may have even forgotten precisely why we do not like blue lamps or why we really like Tupperware. The ego believes that everyone else speaks the same language that they do, or at least they should. If they have difficulty communicating with others it is most definitely the others fault.

We use language to create meaning in our world. It is the only means the ego has to find meaning. It will label everything according to how it is taught to label, it will assign value or lack of value as it does so. This will be the first perceptual filter that will block the child's ability to experience truth. There are many ways to say the same thing. Your particular brand of perception will determine how you chose to describe something. Take, for example, a flower. Some might describe it by assigning a color label to it though no two people might agree on precisely what color it was. Some might describe it from a scientific point of view, give it a Latin label denoting its genus and phylum and perhaps describe the type of environment in which it was likely to grow. Some might call it a weed and become incredibly annoyed with you if you ask them to describe a flower. A mathematician could describe the height of its stalk relative to the length of its petals. Some would describe it in comparison to other types of flowers. Some would write poetry another perhaps a song. You could bring a dozen people before the same flower and find that no two of them described it precisely the same.

With language will come experience. The events of childhood will determine the way the ego will view the rest of its existence. All "new" events will be run through the filter of past events. Music they hear will be compared to the music they heard in their youth. It may be like it and thus good or not like it and thus bad. What is considered to be proper behavior or manners will have been determined. How loudly one should speak in the house, how closely one should stand next to someone with whom they are not intimate, the degree to which eye contact is expected, how one should address their elders. There is tremendous variation among cultures and within them with regard to these mannerisms. The ego is uncomfortable with people who do not observe the same standards of behavior. It believes them to be flawed. They behave incorrectly. They perceive their way as the only correct way of behaving.

Perception is also determined by focus. We choose what we want to pay attention to. The ego chooses what it can make sense of. Two people may go to the same movie. For simplicity sake, let's make it a man and a woman and employ stereotypes (after all the ego loves these). The movie is an action adventure/romantic comedy. The woman (because she is a stereotype) may leave the movie believing it was a beautiful love story. What she remembers are the romantic moments where the two declare their undying love, perhaps she was moved to tears. Stereotypical man, on the other hand, remembers the romantic moment only because it was interrupted by machine- gun fire and was followed by a really good car chase. Their focus was on two different things, though they, in theory, experienced the same event.

Perception is also dependent on the condition of the senses. The functioning of our senses plays an integral role in our ability to interact with the world. Someone whose vision is perfect will see the world differently than someone who is almost blind. Their idea of what the world is, will be shaped by what they see. Two people standing in the same place at the same time may experience two different things solely on the basis of the functioning of their senses, even if they are focusing on the same thing. If one has exceptionally good hearing and is intent on eavesdropping, they may hear every word that is said. It the other has particularly bad hearing but tries equally as hard to hear the conversation, they may only be able to make out some of the words. They may get some of the words wrong. They have a completely different idea of the point of the conversation.

Our perception is also determined by our relative position to the observed event. There is a tremendous difference between standing in front of someone and standing behind them.

All of this is compounded by our brains unwillingness to perceive something as incomplete. It will fill in the blanks for you without you even realizing that that is what has happened. It will hear words that make sense to it though the words were never said. It will complete visual pictures based on what it believes it should be seeing. It sees what it believes it should see, thus it is susceptible to optical illusions. It happily makes animals out of clouds and the face of a man on the moon. They are not there but there is enough for the brain to feel comfortable to fill in the blanks. The problem is we may not all fill in the blanks the same way, and we may in fact fill them in incorrectly.

Our emotional state of being also impacts our interpretation of events. If our day begins by us sleeping through the alarm and we wake to find that we have ten minutes to get to work we may be in a decidedly bad mood for the rest of the day. Our ego is out of sorts from the outset. It is angry at the alarm clock, or the power company if the power went out, or the battery company if the battery backup failed. Because you are angry, the odds increase tremendously of many other things going wrong. You may burn yourself on your morning coffee, your car may not start, if it does you may hit every red light between your home and work. By the time you make it to work your ego may be angry at everything and everyone. It is angry that you are not independently wealthy and are forced to endure mornings such as these. It is angry that your boss will not appreciate you being late. It anticipates the negative comments your co-workers will make. These words that might have been shrugged off on another day may have a much greater impact today. You might think on that day that said co-worker *always* acts like that and forget that on most days you get along just fine. Your focus will be drawn to everything that goes wrong for the rest of the day. Your ego will wonder why these things always happen to you.

Perception and science are at odds with one another. Perception would have us believe that what we do not see is not there and conversely that what we do see is. Thus when the science produced conclusions that did not jive with perception it was science that suffered. The earth is clearly flat; perception can see that this is so. The sun orbits the earth. There is nothing smaller than the eye can see. The ego's perception does not understand the need to question beyond what is readily apparent. It would have you believe that the world is a straight forward orderly place. That life takes place here within the boundaries of shared parameters and there is no need to question that which the eye can see and the brain interprets. It makes the assumption that the interpretation should be the same for everyone.

Consider perception where siblings are concerned. Of any people on the planet, those raised in the same home by the same parents should share the same perspective on life. Words should hold similar meaning; events should be interpreted in the same way. But are they? Do siblings see the world in exactly the same way? A great deal of research has been done on birth order. There are strong tendencies to hold certain ideas based on where you fall in the family hierarchy. Siblings can be extraordinarily different from one another. They can experience the same event, seeing and hearing the same things, yet have a completely different interpretation of what occurred.

Perception runs through multiple filters to deliver us "reality." It tells us that we can interpret the world according to our senses. The ego is certain it has the ability to do this. It is equally certain that we all live in this world, the one it has created. We want to live in a world of black and white, right or wrong. We want to place clearly identifiable labels on everything and live in an orderly world. The problem is, this world exists only for you. No one else lives here. No one else's filtering system works exactly the way yours does. You are alone in the world the ego has created, not even the great love of your life will respond to every outside stimulus the way that you do. Perception creates a world inhabited by a single ego. Here you will live alone no matter the number of people who surround you. You will only see what the ego's parameters allow you to see. It will not allow you to see things it does not believe in. The ego is only capable of belief; it is not capable of truly knowing. There is no truth in perception, though we desperately want there to be.

As we grow, the ego's world becomes less and less comfortable. Again and again it bumps up against other worlds, which in its estimation should not be...and yet they are. To retain some semblance of sanity, the ego must adjust, but that is not its nature. So it must relinquish its hold on some of your thoughts. Every truth you internalize narrows the ego's range of focus. The more you question, the more you recognize that the egos thoughts are impossible to balance, and thus the greater your spiritual growth.

Chapter Four

IN RELATIONSHIP

The ego only exists in relationship to others, without them it is nothing. Without the mirror of the other the ego cannot see itself. It may see the world that its experience has created but it does not know how it fits in. It cannot measure its success or failure without a reference point. Thus the ego is a social creature. It will carefully select the people with whom it chooses to surround itself. They must support its view of self, thus they must be as close as possible to the people who defined it as a child. Yet, the ego is most threatened by people who define themselves in the same way. And so the ego seeks its perfect world, one in which it may know itself by looking at those around it and one which will prevent you from growing past it by keeping it locked in the same conflict it has always known. In this way the ego seeks to ensure that you will only see the person it tells you you have always been.

Part of the ego's job is to tell you if you are generally good or generally bad. Am I the one who obeys the rules or am I the one who does not? The ego's understanding of self will direct it to its place in the world. It will tell you what type of role you are to fill in society, what labels should be attached to you. Are you doctor or lawyer, or are you criminal? These distinctions are made early on. You can watch this happen within families. One child may be identified as the golden child and another as the black sheep. The two can look at one another and know precisely who they are. If you are fortunate to have two children within the same family who identify themselves as reasonably good, they will go to great lengths to take advantage of this when the other sibling is having a moment of misbehavior. While you are scolding one child the other one will be doing the dishes. The child who has never stepped foot into the kitchen will proudly proclaim himself good. He may even go so far as to say it out loud, "look, I am doing the dishes, *I* am a good kid, I am not like my loser brother." He will likely say this loud enough for said loser brother to hear.

Egoic identity is a self-fulfilling prophecy. If those around you believe you are bad and you internalize this belief, you will in fact demonstrate "bad" behavior. This happens regularly in school settings. At very young ages children determine whether or not they can be successful academically in school. It is inevitable that they will draw their own conclusions. Teachers must give feedback to children. If an answer is incorrect it must be corrected for the child to learn. Regardless of how gently this is done, the ego will say to itself. I am wrong. If this is a message that is repeated at home or it they cannot find some success at school they will begin to define themselves as the bad kid or the stupid kid. They will find their niche and thus a means of understanding their identity in negative behavior. If they are going to be the bad kid, then they are going to be very good at being bad. If they are going to be stupid then they will be really stupid.

The ego will also determine your general status with regards to other humans. This does not have to coincide with good and bad, though it may. It will tell you if you are generally superior or inferior to others. It can invent whatever criteria it wants to to reach these conclusions. It can say I get better grades on tests than others; I am superior. It can say I don't get every single answer on the test correct; I am inferior. It can believe that obeying the rules is boring and stupid thus I am smarter than they are for not doing it, I am superior. It can say I obey the rules and behave as best I can because I am frightened to do anything else; I am inferior. All human beings must be ranked in order to know where one falls within the scale. The ego will likely place itself as superior to some, inferior to others. It will congratulate itself for superiority and denigrate itself for inferiority. Most egos prefer the position of superiority and will go to great lengths to preserve this point of view. Within the superior ego there is room to believe that one can do a variety of things well. There is not such room in the inferior ego. Any success is likely to be dismissed as a fluke; compliments will be brushed aside without notice. They do not feel deserved. It does not matter which end of the spectrum the ego finds itself on, either works to push it farther away from the truth that we are all the same. In difference it remains safely within the world it has made. The egos world is thus sustained by judgment; it has good reason to be harsh. It does not matter whether it judges itself or others.

Both the inferior and superior ego will surround

themselves with people who will further that idea. They will gravitate towards that comfortable place where they are disrespected and belittled or the place where they are admired and respected. They will do as egos do and hold those around them responsible for their situation. They will not say that they actively seek out people who are willing to admire them. They will not say they are only comfortable with people who belittle them. An inferior ego will divorce one abusive spouse, swear they will never be involved in that type of relationship again, and turn around and marry the exact same person with a different face. They will not understand how this happened, even if the cycle keeps repeating. The ego cannot break habits because that is all it is. Neither type of ego is willing to take responsibility for its actions though both would claim that they were.

An inferior ego will say it is incapable of creating a positive life for itself which they will likely hold someone else responsible for. The superior ego will assure you that it did everything correctly, someone else made the fatal error. The inferior ego is simply dodging responsibility in a slightly different way. They are not to blame because they are not capable of doing better. Each of these egos is the same in that it has abdicated responsibility for its situation, claiming for whichever reason it was beyond their ability to change it.

Most egos prefer the superior role, and will go to great lengths to defend it, though even an inferior ego believes its world is the correct one. The ego's positive or negative identity is not completely rigid; it can shift depending upon circumstances. We try desperately to avoid these circumstances; they are the places where we are most uncomfortable. We seek out places where we feel we fit, where our skills are either recognized or ignored. Those at either end of this spectrum fall outside of what our society would deem normal. At the superior end is the narcissist, at the other end a person who likely suffered abuse from an early age.

You will seek out people who will reflect back to you what you believe you are. If you remain in the ego's grasp you will find in your life that you keep meeting the same people only in slightly different packages. What you initially believe is a positive relationship will eventually contain all of the same conflicts you have had with people in the past. An ego may go to the extreme step on occasion of isolating itself so that it may say "I am the one who does not need others" but this is a most uncomfortable position for even an ego.

The ego is content to be either good or bad, superior or inferior, what it cannot be is the same. It knows itself *only* in comparison to others. It will spend its life evaluating its relative position to friends, family, co-workers and society as a whole. It will determine its current worth according to how well those around it are doing. It may feel quite good about itself coming home from a day of work where it was recognized for its accomplishments only to turn on the television and be confronted with the rich and famous, to whom it determines it does not so favorably compare. It is likely then to belittle the unfortunate famous one in order to make itself feel better.

The ego will compare its body to societal standards. Is it too fat or too thin? Are its muscles or curves in the proper places? The ego may be more concerned with this than the actual health of the body. It will compare itself financially to those around it and equate money with success. Does it have more or less money than its neighbors or family members? Has it acquired more and better stuff? The ego will be angered by the acquisitions of others. If the neighbor buys a new car than they should have a new car as well. They will see it as a personal affront. Their car has been lessened by the neighbor's new one. They see their body as the sum total of their self. They will judge their own body and others' extremely harshly. If their friend loses weight and gets in shape they will feel that their body has lost value in comparison.

The ego needs to know to what extent is it living in deprivation, for the ego is always living in deprivation. It will never have enough to feel secure because it is not possible for the ego to feel that way. It will forever attempt to find security outside of itself where security does not lie.

The ego looks to others to make it whole. It cannot know itself and as such is incomplete. It does not experience emotion but it believes it should. Truly it is nothing, but you have told it it is yourself. Knowing only insecurity, it searches the world for that which will make it secure. It believes that if it finds the *right* one all its problems will be solved. The two will be as one. Each will meet the other's needs, there will be completion. This is an impossibility for the ego.

When the ego enters into a new romantic relationship, it believes it has finally found what it has always been looking for, someone who will complete it. In fact, it insists that that is the purpose of the other person. The ego will initially see all of the attributes it has been looking for. However, it is looking at them through the filter of its perception and thus will only see what it chooses to see. The problem, of course, is that there are two egos involved in any relationship and each has a very specific idea of who the other should be. Eventually the ego's worlds will collide the ego cannot stay in a state of equality with another for any length of time. They will find that the other does not, in fact, perfectly match up with every need they have or have ever had, or may potentially at some point have. The other may at times behave in a way that is completely and utterly unfathomable. This one, who exists solely for the purpose of your completion, is in fact incapable of fulfilling the task you have appointed it. At this point, the ego will either give way to deeper understanding or establish new parameters for the relationship. The egos can establish a competitive relationship in which each seeks superiority over the other. They may form a relationship where one takes the clear role of superior and the other role of inferior or the relationship will end. If the relationship ends the egos will be dismayed. How could this perfect one who was to fulfill all my dreams have let me down so? How could they not behave in the way that I had set for them? The ego will restart its endless search or may determine that no one will ever meet its needs and become reclusive. Either way, it is the other who has let them down. This is the ego's game. It will happily allow you to carry the pain of loss and rejection from one relationship to another without ever considering that it is itself the common denominator.

That which must compare itself to others in order to know itself, cannot love. In the other's gain, is the ego's loss, this is not love but its opposite. To the ego, to give of oneself is weakness. The ego has nothing to give, it must always conserve, always collect. Though the ego does not possess emotion, when it is firmly in control it directs our emotion. Never is there a connection between the ego and love. It may tell you that it loves but this is not so. The ego can only measure love. All it can tell you is that you have never gotten the love that you deserved. It can recite for you in detail all the times that love has been unfairly withheld. It will convince you that the person you think loves you really does not. It will convince you that you are not in love with the person you thought you were in love with. Love is the ego's ace in the hole. Nothing causes pain like the loss of love. The only thing which sustains the ego is pain. The ego will tell you you must have love, everyone else has it, there is something wrong with you if you don't have a perfect loving relationship. Yet love is the ego's undoing. What it truly wants you to believe is that love is pain. It convinces you not to open yourself up to love because you will get hurt. Ask yourself this question; are there things about you that you would share with no one? The more of these deep dark secrets you hold, the better job your ego has done at convincing you you are unworthy of love. It has convinced you that there is a part of your soul that you can never share. Even the superior ego believes this lie. This is not your soul this is the ego's lie. This is not love, this is not truth. The ego has no relationship to love, thus it has no relationship to truth.

The ego believes it "feels" the way it does because other people control its emotions. Its sees its emotions as completely dependent on outside events. It is lonely because others are not there. It is angry because other people have not behaved the way they should. It is frustrated because events do not transpire as it desires. The ego is not capable of learning from its mistakes because it never makes mistakes, thus it will repeat the same patterns over and over again. What made it angry as a child will make it angry as an adult and will still be someone else's fault. It completely denies its role in any emotional process while still claiming the feelings as its own.

The ego needs others to fail so that it can succeed. Its deepest desire is to be special. In the United States we give free reign to this notion. Value is attached to monetary success and stigma to its lack. We believe that we must be particularly good at something in order to have value. Even if this is just that a person is particularly attractive. We attach no value to ordinary; we must stand out from the crowd. We must have accomplishments that allow us to claim superiority even if it is just for the moment. This supports the ego's agenda well. It knows that it is only a matter of time before someone with greater skill or ability will come along.

The ego can use religion only to set itself apart. It is happy to believe that its particular brand of faith is the only one that is correct and that the vast majority of the people on this planet who do not believe as they do will suffer, at best, annihilation at death. At worst they will be tormented in the pits of hell for eternity. To the ego, this is just. It is the institutionalized belief in superiority.

The ego can take a message of love for all and turn it into love for some. It is not the ego which calls to one's heart, it is a much deeper part of oneself that seeks a connection to God. Ego dominated individuals within a church are often those who have been raised in a particular faith and latched onto its more divisive qualities at an early age. They will stand for division, not for unity, within the Church, the community and the world.

In the Holocaust the ego found its perfect expression. Adolf Hitler knew the ego well. The German people were suffering a national shame. They were forced to surrender in WWI, further shamed by a humiliating peace treaty and suffering from dire economic circumstances. The unemployment rate was extremely high. For most men of this era, the role of breadwinner for the family was their main source of egoic identity. The natural response of the ego under such a heavy load of shame is to redirect emotion to an external source of blame. Hitler knew this, he used it to stir up a Nationalistic furor that measured itself directly by those who were labeled inferior. Not just inferior, but inhuman...cunning, devious responsible for all the indignities the "good" German people had suffered. In the ego's full blown insanity, genocide, carefully planned, was deemed a reasonable "final solution" to a manufactured "problem."

We judge the German people harshly for their horrific deeds. We are sure that under no circumstances would we be capable of such atrocities. Ten million innocent people murdered in cold blood, many of them children. The callous behavior of Nazi soldiers is well documented. It is your ego that tells you you are better than the Nazi soldiers, it is your ego that judges them. All egos are the same. They are acutely sensitive to shame. Any sense of momentary security is obtained at the expense of the inferior "other." Looking outside itself for identity, it is happy enough to let some authority figure tell it who it is. It refuses to take responsibility and will happily relinquish control to leaders. This is what the ego is. Take great comfort in the fact that it is not you.

The ego has no relationship to truth. It will assure you that every bad thing that happens to you is someone else's fault. Every problem in any relationship is again the other's fault. This is the only belief the ego can hold. The world has told it who it is thus the world is responsible for all events that act upon it. The ego's existence lies completely in separation. To believe the world acts upon you, you must believe this is so. The ego can be better than others, it can be worse, it cannot be the same. As I wrote this book, my ego had a lot to say on the subject. One of its favorite loops was, you can't write this book, why would you ever think you could, you should go live in a cave...a small dark one. On days when I felt writing had gone particularly well it told me that I was possibly the most brilliant person who had ever lived. Prophesies should have foretold of my birth. Wise men and women should have gathered at the hospital where I was born. Perhaps there should have been some type of celestial event. Just as quickly it switched back to, you know no one is ever going to read this, why would they? Go back to your cave. If anyone does read this they will laugh at you....and not like you. I keep writing because I know there is no truth in either of beliefs. I know that I am no more than any person, likewise I am no less. I am not special, *I am.*

So long as you think that you *are* ego, it will have full control over your emotional center. The primary emotions you will experience will be negative. Even at times of relative peace, the ego will remind you of things that have gone wrong, perhaps things that happened a long time ago.

If our sense of self is determined by outside forces, we have no self. You could fill a room with people and give them as honest an evaluation of who you are that you could muster. Still they will not agree on who you are... just look at politicians. Some will think you are being honest, some will think you are lying. Some will look at your physical appearance and not listen to a word that you say. Some will judge you by your gender, or your age, or by what social class you appear to belong to. Some will judge you by the color of your skin. Some will judge by your words but words that mean one thing to you may have a completely different meaning to them. Some may be so distracted by other events in their life that they will just fill in the blanks left by their inattention. You are no one if you allow yourself to be defined by others.

Chapter 5

HOLDING FOCUS

Several years ago I stood in my back yard and gazed up at a clear starry sky. I had for the most part stopped doing this. There had been an earlier point in my life when I could stare up at the sky and take comfort in its mystery, I had of late found it most unsettling. I must have been feeling brave that evening to clear my mind and ask the stars for their secret. The answer they gave me was clear and frightening: "you cannot possibly exist" In that instant I knew to the core of my non-existent being that this was true. So, I did what any reasonable human being would do: I went inside and watched television. I felt much better. This is the ego in a nutshell. It is not real; its only hope of continued existence is distraction.

The ego exists only so long as we are willing to let it hold our focus. It must be the center of attention. In order to keep your focus the ego must always have something to say, thus the constant chatter in your mind. It insists on participating in every experience and inventing experience when there is nothing happening. It will use every weapon in its well-stocked arsenal to ensure you that you do not look away from it. So long as you believe its ramblings you will remain locked in its world of insanity. You will believe that lies are truth. The ego must prevent you from knowing a moment's peace. In a quiet moment is its undoing, for in that instant, you might truly see.

The ego insists on being a part of everything. It believes it must interpret every event using linguistic thought. Thus it is forever telling you what you are doing. It will also tell you what other people are doing and be sure to highlight the ways in which their actions interfere with your goals. By insisting on interpreting everything with language, the ego prevents you from having direct experience with anything. You are forever running "reality" through the ego's filter. It can't help but attach layers of labels to everything it encounters. There is a car, it is really expensive, it is blue, it is like one I had in college.

Should you attempt to quiet your mind, perhaps to meditate or pray, the ego will go into overdrive. It will pull out the most distracting (and frequently inappropriate) thought it can come up with. It will then encourage you to feel ashamed of having had that thought at such an inappropriate time. To fight against the ego is only to give it strength. If you say to yourself, I will have no thoughts! Then you are placing your focus precisely where the ego wants it, on itself. To fight against something means to give it your focus. What you give your focus to grows. Your only hope of finding a quieter mind is to redirect your focus. To argue with the ego or become angry with it just feeds it.

The ego has any number of means for preventing a peaceful mind. The ego is the original drama queen. It enjoys trouble and will insist on playing and replaying any stressful event you may have experienced. It will go over and over it, inventing a multitude of alternate scenarios for its outcome. It will examine painful circumstances from every possible angle. Anything to keep you focused on the subject of its choice. The ego will be happy to create drama for you when none actually exists. It will pick fights with people solely to give you something to focus on.

If it cannot find drama in its current external world, it is happy enough to remember old problems. It will replay these for you in vivid detail. The only prompt for this may have been that you simply did not have anything else to think about. The ego loves to remind you of how you have been treated unfairly in the past. It will remind you of how devastating this event was, how badly you were treated. It was not your fault but you will never be able to recover completely from what has been done to you. It may start to replay all of these simply because you were sitting at a red light. Not only will it replay the events, but it will create the emotions that went along with them. Given free reign, you will soon be emotionally re-experiencing the event! You might even start to cry or find that your jaw is clenched, and nothing, absolutely nothing occurred that would give you reason to think about these painful memories. Understand that the ego is not helping you deal with and release these painful thoughts. It is having you re-experience the pain in order to keep it. It does not see the event in a way that would allow you to release it. In order to do this you must be willing to shoulder your share of the responsibility for what happened. You must be able to look at the event from the vantage point of truth. The ego is incapable of that.

Letting the ego run free is like opening a door to a closet stuffed with painful memories. Pretty soon you are remembering every painful moment of your life. You are sad and depressed or angry and on edge simply because for a moment you had nothing to do. If actual memories do not readily come to mind and your life is particularly peaceful at that time, it can invent drama for you. It will happily anticipate the negative greeting you will get from your co-workers that day when you arrive. It might recall a simple comment made by one of them and expand it into a full scale argument you might have with them that day. It can imagine your boss coming to you and firing you, even if there has been no indication that that is likely to occur. It can invent an argument with an imaginary person over an imaginary issue that would be of no actual consequence if it were real. There is no end to its abilities to manufacture problems that require your attention.

There are other less painful options for the ego, it might decide simply to create an alternate reality for you. It will build you a nice house, the house of your dreams. It will create the perfect family. Perhaps it takes the family you have and just tweaks them a bit so that they behave the way it wants them to. It can create whatever future you wish to experience, it can create whatever past. It can imagine the current moment to be completely different than it is. The ego is more than happy to allow you to live in a fantasy world. Fantasy is not truth and is thus perfectly acceptable to the ego. So long as it keeps your mind occupied with false thoughts then the ego is doing its job.

The ego cannot exist within the moment. There it might

find truth and the ego and truth cannot coexist. The ego is happy enough to discuss the future with you. It is not going to go well. There are so many things that could go wrong. The ego will discuss these in detail. People will do things to hurt you and keep you from being successful. There could be natural disasters. You might do something incredibly stupid…that isn't really your fault, but you could still look bad to others. The ego can invent an entire extended future for you based on everything going wrong. Or some things could go right for a while and then go wrong. This is worse because you will, in the ego's estimation, feel more pain by loss. The ego does not believe it is better to have loved and lost. It firmly believes it is just better to suffer so that you won't somehow suffer more from loss.

The ego will happily live in the past. It keeps a catalog of events to remind you of, the more painful the better. It will reinvent the past and project for you a new future. If the ego is paying attention to the moment, it is not enjoying it. It is there but it has distanced itself by judging the moment as somehow unsatisfying. It has determined that this is not where I want to be and not what I want to be doing. It looks forward to the moment when it will have what it wants and dismisses the current moment that it does not want.

The ego dwells in the past or frets about the future or worries about the current situation. It seeks to fill every moment with chatter. So long as you are listening to its endless litany you are not truly experiencing what is right in front of you. The ego is never happy, it always wants more. It wants more from the past. It will dwell endlessly on injustices, on painful moments, wanting them to have been different. It will remember events you enjoyed and find fault with them. It will replay every slight you have experienced in its attempt to keep your mind from true experience. With the present moment it will also find fault. Its insistence in participating in every experience will limit your experience of everything. It must label everything; it cannot simply let things be. It far prefers negative labels to positive ones.

The ego always assumes that some type of deprivation is just around the corner, if it is not being immediately experienced. It is thinking about the next bite of food before you have swallowed the one you are chewing. If you have money in the bank it tells you that you need more, you could lose that money and then you would not have enough. The ego is quite adept at using fear to hold your focus. It tells you you must think about what could cause you harm. It tells you that if you do not think about this you will suffer. The ego pays close attention to every negative story it hears, all the more to keep you worried about. It likes to tell sad stories. It picks out all of the worst stories in the newspaper and somehow manages to relate them to you. Its message is clear: You are vulnerable, be afraid. If you are frightened enough you might be able to stay safe. Be afraid that you might have cancer, worry that you cannot pay your bills, and think about all the things that could go wrong all of the time. This is the way the ego likes it best. So long as it convinces you to be frightened while simultaneously telling you it can keep you safe the ego can believe it has some semblance of security.

The ego's best weapon against security is fear. It would

happily keep you in a state of fear. The news plays to the ego on a daily basis. Murder, destruction, mayhem of one sort or another, these are the headlines. This is what sells; the worse the news, the better the profit margin. The ego's greatest fear is loss. Because it is afraid of loss, it is terrified of gain. The more that is gained, the greater potential there is for loss. Nowhere is this truer than with regards to love. The ego is incapable of experiencing love but believes it must be obtained. It is the fear of love's loss that sustains it. Nothing is more terrifying to the ego than the loss of a loved one. The ego defines itself largely according to the ones it believes it loves. Their loss thus diminishes itself.

It holds over you its ultimate weapon, death. One day, you will cease to be. You may believe that you will go on in one state or another but what you now know, will be entirely lost. The ego's only power lies in its ability to marshal emotion. In emotion there is far more truth, but emotion guided by ego is misled. So long as the ego goes unquestioned, emotion will follow its lead. When this is the case, the ego controls all actions. The greatest power the ego has is over what it believes to be itself, the body. An inferior ego will suffer a myriad of illnesses and injuries, always attributing them to outside circumstances. A superior ego will suffer stress related illnesses. Anger takes a heavy toll on the body. A superior ego will spend a great deal of its life angry at those who do not live up to its expectations.

The ego is perfectly willing to engage in mindless distraction. It will watch endless hours of television without processing a single thought. It will play video games; it can do any number of tasks without ever participating in them. This is the difference between mindlessness and purpose. A task completed with purpose carries with it a positive emotion.

The ego is not evil but from it comes what we call evil in this world. It does what we have asked it to do; it distracts us from the pain we have chosen not to see. It repeats the lie we have chosen to live by, if I do not see it, it is not there. And if I do see it, it must be. It is in all things a contradiction; the ego is not capable of rational thought. It believes we are in need of God's love but that we must be special in order to deserve it. It sees God as measuring love because that is the only way the ego can understand it.

The ego is engaged in an endless and impossible search for itself. You have told it that it is you and that you must be able to understand yourself. It has no choice but to see a world of separation. It sees endless variety in its mission to rank and order. It looks for itself in the only place it believes is real, the external world. The ego cannot see unity and thus the ego can never see love. In love we are one, the ego can be one with nothing.

The ego causes only pain, it offers only limitations. It will always be found wanting, never satisfied. It follows its endless path to self-destruction. It is a foregone conclusion. The ego's influence is quite evident in our world. It is the voice that says we are not safe. In order to be safe we must attack those who might wish to destroy us. The ego encourages the preemptive strike. The ego says that if you are hurt, you must hurt back. But understand that there are no circumstances under which the ego will be satisfied. A country can never have enough weapons, not even if it could destroy the earth ten times over. A country can never have enough wealth; the next great depression will surely come. We must, says the ego, be ever vigilant to protect ourselves. To relax would surely mean the end because there is always someone out there waiting to take advantage of a moment's weakness. This is the world the ego has made.

Part II-

THE SUBCONSCIOUS

Chapter 6

THE SUBCONSCIOUS

We are our emotions. That is the true core of our being. How we feel about our self is how we experience the world. In truth there is only one emotion which is love. We have lost sight of this and so what we experience is love's loss. Every emotion we have is either grounded in love or in its absence. Every action we take is determined by our emotions. Every action we take is to restore love. We all want to feel good; we have just become so very confused about how to go about this. We may live in a mansion and have more money than we could ever spend but if we are not happy it does not matter, we will still be looking for something we do not have. The ego will tell us that what we need to feel happiness is outside of ourselves. The ego cannot see that it seeks the impossible by looking outside for what is within.

We separate ourselves from love by creating artificial divisions in our mind. To the ego we have given our focus and what we believe is thought. We call all of the words which run through our crowded mind our thoughts. We keep our emotions in a separate compartment so that we can believe we are keeping our true self safe. Here we can hide that which we feel is too painful to fully experience. Our subconscious is our emotional center. At the root of the subconscious is our heart, the term used in Western countries to refer to our deepest feelings. The heart can only know love or believe in its absence. Thus the heart may know a glimmer of universal love or it will experience its loss and feel pain. As the subconscious moves away from its center and towards the ego, other emotions will be found there. These are the ego's weapons against truth. Here you will find fear and anger. The subconscious is an emotional continuum which runs from emotions which completely deny truth (fear and anger) to those which approach truth, either love or loss. Our spiritual journey, which will hold many experiences, takes us from one end of the continuum to the other. At the end of our journey we will find truth.

In order to create a divided mind, in order to separate that which is one, we must believe what is not true. At its core, the subconscious holds one false idea. It is this thought that divides our mind and this thought that separates us from God. It is a terribly painful thought, one so devastating that we would rather suffer the torments of hell on earth rather than face it…and so we do.

Imagine for a moment, that you have the perfect spouse. If you are fortunate to have someone in your life that is close to that description, use that person but remove any old hurts or annoying imperfections that may at times come between the two of you and bliss. Remember how it felt when you first met this person, how life was different for a time. If you have children, remember their birth.

How for an instant there was such love and hope for the future. Imagine now that this is what life is always. You are surrounded by perfect love, from your spouse, your children, and friends. Everyday holds only promise.

Now it is gone. It is gone because you made a mistake. Your spouse, your children, your friends have perished at your hand. You are alone. You can no longer feel their love, only its loss. You had perfection, now you have nothing but shame. Do you still believe in love or do you believe in loss? This is who we are. Beings that once had everything but now can focus only on its loss. We have chosen to substitute this thought for Truth. Though we believe the thought, it is too painful for us to look at directly. We believe its truth while attempting to hide from its pain. Thus we create a division between thought and emotion. Thought becomes the distraction from pain and we accept absurd levels of torment in its place. We torture ourselves, each other, our world in a desperate attempt to avoid that which we believes is our deepest truth, that we are unworthy of love, that we have lost perfect love because of our own "sin." We believe at our core that this is so. So long as we keep running, spinning, kicking, spitting, we think we may forget. We look to the ego, we may look to God, but we do not want to look at the error that keeps us here. Even when one makes the choice of uncompromising self-examination, it is difficult to let go of this idea. We have been taught from childhood that to say that we are extraordinary is to be arrogant, that the only way to achieve value is to be special. We must somehow convince ourselves that this is not so. We are extraordinary and we are not special, we are one beautiful being of love and light that needs only to remember itself. To give up the crazy notion that love can be lost. We *are* love, to believe it can be lost is to lose ourselves and so here we are….lost.

We have told ourselves this story since time began. The story of original sin is a central tenant in three of the world's major religions. In the Garden there was no separation between us and God, and there was no shame. The acquisition of shame and its effect on the relationship between God and man is mentioned specifically in the story. In the Garden there was no loss, all needs were met, and there was no want. But this is not a story with a happy ending. Something comes into the Garden that was not there before. The snake is the ego, the voice that tells you, you need more than what you already have. In the Garden Adam and Eve had everything, but the snake told them they had been denied. They needed something more, that they did not have enough. The snake convinces them they need to take a bite of the forbidden fruit and provides them a scapegoat so that they do not have to take personal responsibility for their decision. They can blame the snake, or better yet, Adam can blame Eve. Women have borne the brunt of the ego's desire to shift blame almost since civilization came into existence and in some societies it continues even today.

When Adam and Eve ate the forbidden fruit what they acquired was the knowledge of good and evil. Until this time they had known only love. Now they saw opposing forces, not love but separation. No longer were they one with everything in existence, they were individuals diminished by their own choice. They had lost their true self and accepted a flawed being in its place. They were shame locked in bodies' form. They hid themselves from God when he came to the garden, covering the body they now believed was naked with leaves. The story tells us that God cast us out of the garden; this is not so. We removed ourselves from paradise by believing in separation and believing we had chosen self over God. For this we believe we are undeserving of God's love, that we should bear the burden of our sin for eternity. Human beings internalized this belief and locked it carefully away in the recesses of their mind. What we do not see is that this is the ego's God. One who says I cannot have others be like me. I must be superior to all. No one can share my knowledge or I will no longer have value.

The first written story, chiseled into stone thousands of years ago, was the Epic of Gilgamesh. It is a common enough story of a hero and his adventures. Within the story is a tale familiar to many cultures, the story of a great flood. A flood sent by the gods, who had found their creations lacking, with the intention of wiping out mankind. The story is repeated in similar fashion in the old testament of the Bible, as well as in many other cultures. It is one of our most enduring stories. We believe that God should judge us and that we will be found guilty.

We are a culture that has traditionally focused on the punishment of misdeeds rather than positive proactive intervention. We spend far more money on building prisons than on schools and programs for young people that might prevent them from going to jail in the first place. For Christians the sinful nature of mankind is never in question. The Bible makes it clear that our nature is so sinful that a perfect sacrifice was required to atone for us, so that those of us who carefully follow a circumscribed set of rules can be forgiven. This, so long as you have chosen the correct set of rules. But is it the reward of heaven or the fear of hell that drives us? If we do not follow the rules to our maker's satisfaction or have the misfortune to have aligned ourselves with the wrong set, we will suffer for eternity.

We find it far easier to hang on to negative thoughts than to positive ones. At the end of the day it is the negative events we tend to dwell on, but we do not like to feel emotional pain. We would do anything to avoid this suffering. The ego does its best to provide distraction for you. Its first effort will be at deflection. Be angry it says, it is someone else's fault. Someone else's behavior caused you to feel this way. It will go over and over and over the incident in an attempt to make it something different than what it was. Perhaps if I could find another way to look at it, I could see that it was not my fault and I would not need to feel badly. Of course the repetition of the event serves the ego's purpose as well, it keeps you stuck on this one event and feeling badly about it. It may take another tack and try and create some completely unrelated fantasy scenario in which you are the hero of the day... and everyone loves you. The ego will do whatever it takes to keep your attention.

When we experience pain, gut-wrenching, heart-stopping loss, what we truly experience is not that something or someone has been lost, but that it has been taken away. Not by random events but by a force which has targeted our heart. The ego will rant and rave, it will seek to blame, it will rage at the injustice. Blame may fall in many different places. A mother may blame herself for the cancer that takes her child, a father blame himself for his inability to fix it. They may blame each other, or the doctors, or a society that lives with high levels of carcinogens. They may choose to allow anger to fill their aching heart. Yet, when the pain is at its most raw, when the ego has exhausted its rants for just a moment, the heart cries out to God or fate unknown to justify the loss of this precious one. We may not believe in God in the quiet times of our life but when we have lost what we believed to be a part of our self we at some point believe that God has taken them from us. At our most honest, raw, painful moment, we will ask why. In the asking, a portion of the answer is implied. We believe the answer is centered in ourselves. We have done something that has caused God to take from us what we held most dear. We believe we are being punished for our sins regardless of our ability to understand them.

We are so willing to hold on to pain because it matches our core human emotion. Because we hold the idea that we are unworthy, we are far more likely to focus on insult rather than compliment. It is not truth but it is what we hold on to, an idea in which we believe. Most of us do not enjoy making mistakes in front of other people, even if they are of little consequence. Some of us will live for an extended period of time in the shadow of that mistake. It is an enlightened soul that can make a very public error and brush it aside knowing that it does not truly reflect upon their being. We judge ourselves harshly; we are more than willing to tell ourselves that we are of no value, even if we would not accept this judgment from others. This does not come from the ego, it comes from our heart. We tell our self our relationship ended because we are unworthy of love. We tell our self that we have no friends (regardless if this is so) because no one would want to be our friend. Most of us do not dwell in this dark place for long periods of time, but it is there. Self-doubt lives in all of our hearts. It may lie dormant for long periods of time, but when we get an emotional kick in the gut, we begin to hear its whispers. That which could not possibly be our fault, somehow is. If we did not hold on to self-doubt which is shame, we could not suffer emotional pain. To doubt oneself is to diminish one's self, this is shame. If this were not so we would know ourselves whole and complete regardless of circumstances.

Focus determines experience. Our ability to experience love is dependent upon the amount of pain we have stored in our subconscious. If there is a great deal of pain here, we will look to the ego to provide us protection. Most of us believe that we should love and be loved in return and so we will attempt to find some semblance of it in this world. The problem is, we look to our heart, which resides at the root of the subconscious. The heart believes in loss, it can be broken. It is far easier to shift focus back to the ego when this occurs than it is to remain with this painful experience until it can be released. In this physical plane of existence we believe that love may come and go, that we can love someone one day but fall out of love with them the next. We believe there are degrees of love, or different kinds of love for different people. There is the love we feel for friends, the love we have for family, love for our children and romantic love. This is love in separation. It is but a shadow of God's love.

Our focus is quite capable of shifting from ego to heart and back to ego again, throughout your life and from one moment to the next. Whenever experience becomes what you deem too difficult to bare, the ego is waiting to comfort you. As our life unfolds, there is great potential to learn to trust yourself and to rely less on the ego's distractions. If all goes well your life will be a stream of events that steadily disconnects you from ego. Understand that this is entirely your choice. You choose how to respond to painful events. Most of us require many bumps in the road in order to learn who we are. We are a stubborn lot.

The subconscious exists only because we hold on to the idea that we are unworthy of our Father's perfect love. We believe he has deemed us unfit for paradise, cast us out of the Garden and left us to suffer for our sins. Many of us hold out hope that if we carefully adhere to our religions dogma, there is a chance for redemption. We may be saved from our sinful nature. We believe in the original sin, if we did not, we would not be here. We would not require this plane of existence in order to learn our way past the original mistake.

We believe that within us is a place of darkness that light cannot touch. We may live our entire life without realizing we hold this thought or we may live our life embracing fully the notion that our soul is black. For many of us it is just the vague idea that there are some things about us which we would never share with others. Some recurring thoughts, deep desires of the less than noble kind or barely contained or uncontained intent to do harm to others. We do not share ourselves fully with each other, we humans; we always hold some part of ourselves back. We believe our existence depends on individuality and individuality requires a clear separation between self and others.

Chapter 7

EGO AND EMOTION

As infants we are spirit only, but we are spirits that believe in loss. Thus we hold a false idea which creates a space within our mind which is willing to believe that which is untrue. Because of this when an infant experiences imbalance it experiences loss. Its stomach was full but now it is empty, it was comfortable but now its diaper is wet. An infant must have its balance restored by an outside force. Not only does it believe in loss, but it has yielded its power to restore balance to another. As a child grows it is meant to learn to reverse this process. It learns it must be responsible for restoring its own balance. It learns through lifetimes that loss is not Truth. Loss is only a belief we have allowed our focus to rest upon. In order to learn this you must come to understand what you are and how you alter yourself through personal preference.

Our emotional center, our heart, becomes tied to external circumstances before the ego comes into being. In fact, it is only because of this that the ego will be needed. At some point in the first year of life a child develops what is called object permanence. This is the understanding that though they can no longer see something, it is still there. It may be under the blanket or in another room, but it has not disappeared. Rather than be comforted by permanence, what the child now perceives is loss. What it once had can be taken from it. The child will now begin to attach its emotional well-being to the external circumstances surrounding it. For it to be happy it must have the things it has attached value to. Children will vary greatly in the degree to which they need the world to conform to their wishes. They may insist that mother be with them always and that no other care giver will do. They may develop a strong attachment to a stuffed animal or blanket and insist that these be readily available at all times. Misplace or lose this object, or lovey, and you will experience full scale rejection of the moment.

At a preverbal, pre-ego, point of development the child has already externalized its concept of self. It is only willing to see itself as OK if its world is in proper order. The child's heart will be open to love only when its world convinces it that it is safe to do so. We need the world to support our concept of self only because we believe in loss. If you hold no be such belief, if you believe in yourself entirely, you have no such need. If you know that you are whole and complete always, the external world can be as it is with no emotional effect on you.

By acquiring preference you limit your being. You say that I will accept this set of circumstances but not those. The greater limits you place on acceptance, the more of the world you exclude from yourself and the narrower your focus. You diminish yourself by refusing to accept things as they are and insisting that they should be different. You essentially lock yourself in a state of shame, or diminished self. Your heart believes that to reject that which you cannot control, or make as you would have it be, is to protect itself from loss. That which has already been rejected cannot be lost. It has already been preemptively denied. As a child grows it learns there are many things in the world that can be taken away from it. It tries to create a world in which it can be safe and in so doing denies most of the world.

In denying the world it has denied itself. Implicit in this decision is the belief that the heart cannot handle loss. This is self-doubt and there is no more destructive force on earth. If we do not believe in ourselves we must reject our world as we reject our self. The focus on fear of loss, maintains the state of separation from True self. The desire to no longer suffer the state of shame (loss) causes the shift in focus from loss to the ego's distraction.

As a child grows he or she will inevitably experience circumstances that do not align with its sense of well-being, and the child suffers emotional pain. The ego grows along with the pain as the child looks increasingly to it for protection. With the growth of verbal abilities the ego begins to establish its connections to the child's emotions. It builds thought patterns to support emotional responses. By using language to explain the child's emotions to itself it begins to place a barrier between the child and its true feelings. The heart does not speak with words, its thoughts are felt, thus the ego and the heart can never be one. The ego chooses words to explain emotion that it believes will protect the child from pain. It begins to shape emotion. It uses anger to cover painful events which have occurred and fear to prevent painful events in the future. The child's tender heart takes shelter in the only place it can be found. The more pain a child experiences the greater hold the ego will take and the greater the distortion between egoic thought and emotion.

Take a moment to consider the happy memories you hold from your early childhood. They have a different quality to them than memories stored later in life. Remember how you could experience a day as if you had never seen a day before. As if it held magic. You could almost wear it as if it were you. A beautiful sun shiny day, a rainy snuggly day you could wrap yourself in. These memories hold joy, true joy. They hold the nature of experience before the ego took control of your perception. They are memories in which you can truly see.

The more pain an ego deals with, the more adept it becomes at deflection. Pain deflected is pain denied. Pain which is not truly experienced is stored at the level of the subconscious. The more pain that resides here, the less able one is to connect with their true spirit. The subconscious, which originally held one false idea, now holds all of the pain the ego has told you not to feel.

The subconscious holds your personal truth, that which you believe about yourself on an emotional level that you may not even be aware of. Held deeply here, hidden away by the ego, are ideas that may go long unexpressed by words. This idea of who you are will likely be fully formed before you are a teenager. It will hence forth tell you what you can do and what you cannot do. It will tell you what talents you may have and which ones you do not. You will have acquired these ideas in small part through experience but mainly by what other people have told you is true. The ego will essentially have created a false emotional state to support its idea of self. If you played the piano as a child and someone of importance to you told you it was the most beautiful sound they had ever heard, you may go to your grave believing you are a talented pianist, even if you never find another that holds that opinion. If, on the other hand, someone of importance told you that they were tired of listening to that noise, it does not matter what talent you might have had, you will likely decide to no longer play. Most importantly, your heart will have decided what degree of value you hold in this world. The ego will happily provide repetitive loops of verbal thought to support your hearts conclusions. The heart does not express itself with words, it does so with feelings. If you believe you are a good pianist you will have positive feelings about it and thus continue to play. If you believe you are not a good pianist you will have negative feelings about it and thus cease to play. These are the thoughts of your heart. It is the ego that feels it must put these feelings into words but the ego runs its own agenda. It will choose words based on its understanding of the outside world, not on the inside world. Thus the ego is not a true reflection of your feelings and in fact, exists to deny them.

This point at which your ego and emotions are in balance, regardless of the degree of truth that is there, is like a set point. This is your place of comfort, though it may be a terribly uncomfortable place. You may live in this place for the rest of your life or move past it only to return to it at times of distress. You will, without knowing why, seek circumstances that match your set point. If you grew up in world of chaos, then you will seek chaos. If you grew up in an abusive home you will seek to either be the abuser or the abused. You will not know why or how you wind up in the circumstances you believe you wish to escape. The ego may say for a time," I do not deserve this, I should be treated better", but this does not match the beliefs of the heart and it does not matter what the ego says when it is not in balance with the heart. The subconscious will always succeed in re-establishing its set point, so long as the ego does its job and keeps you from looking at truth.

The ego is highly flawed; it is incapable of sound logic. It employs anger as a defense against the pain of not getting what you wanted, yet anger itself becomes a barrier to getting what you want. As the ego clashes with truth you may learn to believe in truth. As you accept greater truth, you narrow the ego's domain and begin to clear some of the emotional clutter it has stored. A space is created between ego and emotion, where self-reflection may occur. The more one is willing to place focus on self-reflection the greater their potential to grow past the ego's influence.

This is a skill we hope to develop in early adulthood. It can however, make for a difficult and confusing time period. It can feel as if we are of two distinctly separate minds. The ego may say "I am going to college" because that is what the ego believes will garner it the respect of others, but if the subconscious is not in agreement there will be failure at one point or another. If you do not believe from an emotional point of view that you have the ability to be a college student then you will not be able to succeed. When failure occurs the ego will begin running all of the old scripts to protect and distract from the painful truth of failure. It will be everyone else's fault, professors, friends, significant others, parents, former teachers, even God. The ego and the subconscious are now again in alignment.

The only way to alter one's set point is a willingness to look honestly at oneself. It is first helpful to recognize the ego for what it is, distraction. As long as you allow it to fill every moment with endless drivel, the vast majority of your thoughts will be a meaningless repetition of previous experience. Every "new" thing you see will be evaluated according to the same old filter. You will need to take a step back from the ego. Watch it for a time, begin to understand its habits and let them point you in the direction of your true self. Ask yourself how you developed this pattern of thought. Note the connection between thought and emotion. You must honestly question your emotional responses and corresponding thoughts. Is there truth within them or did you long ago store false ideas? Did someone tell you as a child that you were of no value? This is false, it does not matter who you are or what you have done in your life, you are of great value.

As a person continues to age their emotions move steadily away from the ego's control, we refer to this as emotional maturity. The more mature an individual, the less hold the ego has. False emotions are released from the subconscious and we get closer to a true understanding of self. Sometimes this happens with the help of a therapist; always it occurs with a determination to face truth. With growth will come imbalance. A child's body is the perfect metaphor for this. There will be some distinctly awkward points of physical maturation, times when a child may be all arms and legs. Imbalance is a natural part of growth. It may be temporarily uncomfortable but well worth it in the end. Our natural state is peace and joy, action and inaction, always in the direction of growth. Love must give of itself to be love. Peace and joy are only aspects of love. In peace we rest and are in balance, in joy we extend ourselves and are temporarily out of balance. When you do not hold the belief in loss, joy is a miraculous state of imbalance from which you can only gain.

Chapter 8

LOVE AND LOSS

All of the pain we suffer in our lives comes from the denial of love. All pain is the original pain of the loss of our true self; it is the loss of our own sense of well-being or wholeness. The love we at times manage to hold in our heart is but a fragile piece of eternal love, yet it is enough to remind us of what we have lost. We know that in this life it does not matter on whom we chose to bestow love; they will one day be gone. And so our heart which so desperately aches to open itself to love remains closed to all but loves smallest pieces, those over which we imagine we might exert some control. A heart which knows only love knows only peace and joy, never sadness, never pain. We do not believe this is so and so we allow the ego to martial our emotions substituting fear in the place of joy, and anger in the place of peace. We do this because we believe this is the only way we can stay safe.

Our world is dominated by fear. When the heart says, I do not have what I need, the ego says I am afraid I will not be able to get what I want and it creates a state of anxiety. It masks the heart's sense of emptiness with fear.

A person living with anxiety may not realize it comes from the level of the heart, not the mind. It is a state of being without what is perceived to be needed. The ego will translate this into the need for externals. It will say there is not enough money to be secure or we do not have enough possessions or those that we have are in jeopardy of being lost. The ego would prefer you live believing that destruction is just around the corner than that you feel the pain residing in your heart.

In order to ensure that you will live in this state constantly, when the heart says I am happy, I feel love, the ego says you will lose it, it cannot last forever and your heart will begin to close to love. It is the belief in love's loss that causes the loss of love. The ego will then create expectations for the future that will insure you remain safely afraid. It is a twisted attempt to circumvent loss by insuring there is no gain. Here the heart is in agreement, it has already said I do not have what I need. The ego uses expectations to effect outcome. It may say expectations must be kept low in order to avoid disappointment, therefore effecting outcome by limiting the possibility of success. It may set the expectations exceedingly high; well beyond what the heart believes is in the realm of possibility, therefore ensuring disappointment. Either way the ego has achieved its goal, it has limited your being. It has kept a state of well-being from settling in your heart.

There are those who would argue that fear is a good thing, that it is necessary to keep us safe. This is not so, the purpose of fear is to hold us back from experiencing truth. It is quite possible to make reasonable decisions regarding safety without being afraid. You can stand at the edge of a cliff and choose not to jump because you do not want to die rather than because you are afraid. There will be those who would argue that fear has been a necessary step in our physical evolution. That the fight or flight response helped us to survive in harsh conditions. But did it? Does allowing your mind to be filled with fear encourage clear thinking? Are you likely to see the best possible solution to a problem when you are afraid? If you are standing face to face with a hungry saber tooth tiger is fear going to help you escape. Will fear think to pick up the large stick that happens to be sitting at your feet? Will fear remember the small cave you just passed and might be able to squeeze into before big and toothy pounces? Is it necessary to experience fear to direct all of your body's reserves to escape or is this simply a byproduct of intense focus? Athletes competing at high levels push their bodies to performances often unattainable in training situations. Their bodies produce adrenaline in response to their focus on the task at hand. They are not afraid because if they were, they would not succeed. The seed of doubt would have been planted in their mind and this is all it takes to undermine even the most skilled athlete.

When the heart lives in a continual state of deprivation it will say, I have *never* had what I needed. The ego will see whomever or whatever is standing in front of it as proof that this is so. It does not matter if this is a stranger or one who is well known, the ego says they are responsible for all the longing the heart has ever known. When the ego speaks it will be angry, it will say "you always do this" or "this always happens to me." The ego believes it has found itself in unfair circumstances yet again. It insists that these be made right and so it rages at those around it. It screams.

"you must behave the way I want you to behave, I can only have what I need if you behave correctly, the world must be the way I want it to be". The ego is measuring current circumstances against predetermined criteria. Long ago the heart decided what it needed to feel love and established its preferred state of being.

People vary tremendously in their preferences. The degree of importance you place on them will determine how deeply you feel loss if they are not met. We all know people whose sense of self hangs in a delicate balance, whose life is forever being turned upside down by what they perceive as the hand of fate. These people have a narrow range of tolerable experiences. Virtually every moment may be painful to them because it does not hold precisely what they would choose for it to hold. We are all like this to one extent or another.

When we experience anger, the heart says I have never had what I have needed and the ego places the blame on the one it finds in front of it. An angry ego says that I have always felt this way or you always behave this way. This is because anger is attached to the past. The heart is at its most anguished, those who carry a great deal of anger in their subconscious have known very little love, even if it has been offered. The heart speaks the truth; the ego twists it into blame. Anger hides the deepest pain, it is an effective diversion but can only lead to self-destruction. It does not matter who is standing in front of them, a stranger or a friend, they have, perhaps innocently, triggered the heart to remember what it believes it has never had.

We attempt to circumvent loss by holding tightly to our preferences in the belief that they will also limit our experience of loss. By insisting on keeping our focus on that which we do not want, we continually experience what we do not want. We experience pain when events do not go as we want them to, events do not meet our expectations. The farther they fall from our expectations, the greater the pain. We perceive that we have been lessened. We are willing to love when experience meets expectation, but unwilling to do so when it does not. We are therefore closer to our true self in times of joy and far less so in times of sorrow. What we experience as pain is further loss of self.

Preference is itself a withholding of love. You may love some people under certain circumstances (when they behave as you would have them behave) and other people under no circumstances. By withholding love, you withhold yourself. You think you withhold love because some people are undeserving of it. In Truth you withhold love because you are afraid it will not be returned. You are afraid that giving love means risking losing a part of yourself. We withhold love because we see a world that is undeserving of love. It is the withholding itself that creates the world we see. We want love but fear its loss. It is fear that prevents us from having what we want. If you do not allow yourself to experience universal love, than you will experience love with limits…loss. Your actions are determined by your emotions. If you believe in loss, your actions will be guided by this belief and you will experience loss. It is this simple. What you believe is true, is what will be in your life.

All actions are centered in love. Our behavior is determined by emotion. When we chose a course of action it is because of the way it makes us feel. If we are afraid of love, we choose actions whose purpose is to cover the pain of living disconnected from our true self. We may be angry much of the time. Anger is the most effective way to cover both fear and pain. It provides a temporary sense of power. The more out of control the anger, the more the situation and all involved in it, centers on the display. You cannot ignore a person who is enraged and using violence as a means of control. For the moment, anger is in control. But this is short-lived; the human body can only maintain rage for a short period of time. Once it has passed, the body is spent and must rest. This intense an emotion leaves one exhausted.

Because we believe that love is loss, we all, with the exception of the enlightened few, attempt to experience love in ineffective and temporary ways. We have certain behaviors we use as substitutes. We may place our focus on eating, or drinking, shopping or playing golf. We may insist that our latest purchase make us happy and it may, at least for a while. Then another purchase will have to be made. Every action that human beings take is an attempt to restore love to their heart. The person who rages at the world is screaming "Love me! Love me! Love me!..dammit!" The person who drinks themselves into oblivion is attempting to escape the painful absence of love from their heart. The person who eats too much is trying to bring comfort to an aching heart. We all want to feel good, regardless of whether we call this love. Yet, even positive emotion we feel is a shadow of eternal love and every pain is of its loss. When we seek to feel good, we seek our true self. There is no greater feeling of emptiness than not knowing one's self. This is a state in which many of us live. No one takes action with the conscious thought, "this is really going to hurt." The ego twists our thoughts and actions to support its own agenda. It is the fear of love and the pain of its loss that causes us to allow the ego to pretend to be our self. We are afraid of our true self, thus we are willing to embrace distraction in fear's place.

The disconnect between heart and egoic mind can leave one completely out of touch with their emotions. They may find themselves intensely angry but have no real idea of why. When we experience pain, the ego jumps in as quickly as possible with deflection. It does not give the heart a chance to fully process and release the event. Because of this expectations remain the same as before the event occurred. Consider this with regards to the death of a loved one. If the ego is allowed to step in and deny this loss, future expectations will not be altered. Thus the heart will live in a constant state of expecting that person to be there which will result in a constant state of loss. The heart will feel that it never has what it wants and the ego will replace this with anger.

You believe in loss, the ego ensures loss. You believe that love is pain; the ego seeks to avoid pain and so must avoid love. It is a vicious cycle, this relationship between heart and the ego's mind. The ego seeks to protect the heart and in so doing locks it in perpetual loss. We say that we want love but we do not know it's true nature. It is the act of withholding love that diminishes you. It is the belief that love and loss can be one and the same that leaves our world such a wretched mess. When we recognize that love abides within us, that the nature of love is extension and that giving love can only result in more love do we have the hope of freeing ourselves from this prison of perception.

The ego and the heart look at love the same in one very important way. They both believe that to experience it is to be special. The ego measures love, this is the only thing it can do. It says I have more love than others or I am loved by someone who is better than the person that loves you. Or it may say no one loves me, no one ever will, I am not special, I am ordinary. Ordinary to both the ego and the subconscious is not to be loved. Both believe that love is a temporary state to be acquired and held as long as possible but both believe that love has a beginning and an end.

Romantic love, we believe, is a special type of love to be experienced by only two people. If the great love of your life told you that they loved you with all of their heart and soul but that they loved another in exactly the same way, you would be devastated. To feel love fully, your heart believes it must be the only recipient of that particular love. Sibling rivalry stems from exactly this belief. Here is one of the few circumstances where we say that all should be loved the same. A parent should not have one child that they love more than another, but children do not want to be loved in the same way as another, they want to be special. They want to say "look at me, Mom or Dad" and be told how great they are, what a clever thing only they can do. If they cannot fill the role of the favorite child, then they may decide to take the role of the black sheep. If they believe they are not the favorite than they may choose to be special, distinct and different in another way. That this type of special lacks love will likely lead to a more painful existence for this child but they have avoided what we all dread, the anonymity of being the same.

We chose not to believe that there is only one love and that it is eternal. Instead we believe that we can acquire some love here from one relationship, more love in another place from a different relationship. If we are fortunate we can hold on to multiple types of loving relationships at the same time, at least for a while. We categorize and label love. We believe there is romantic love, familial love, the love of friends, love between parent and child. We believe it is different because we place different expectations upon different types of relationships. We expect these relationships to meet our needs in different ways. What we know for certain is that we want and need love. We believe as humans we must acquire it from others who are separate from ourselves. The heart knows God's love but it has taken on the belief that we are undeserving of it and must exist without it. It has distorted the nature of love and cast us into a world where love will always result in loss.

In Truth we are creatures of Love. That love is the entirety of our being has been only temporarily forgotten. It is the acquisition of love that drives our every action upon this earth. Whether it be a move towards love or a fearful retreat from it, love is the core of our being. In seeking love, we seek our true selves. All of the pain we suffer on this earth comes from our denial of love. When we hold personal preference, we prevent ourselves from experiencing our true self. So long as we withhold love from anything, we withhold ourselves.

Chapter 9

ENERGY

We are beings of pure energy, the energy of consciousness. We chose at our current level of consciousness to manifest ourselves as physical beings. We make this choice unconsciously, not realizing that we have made a decision at all. As physical beings we are still the energy of consciousness. When our being begins to match that of universal consciousness, we call it love. We feel that all is right. We do not know it is simply because we are experiencing a shadow of our true self. When we do not experience love, we are in a state of denial of self. We deny love. We have forgotten we are love and believe instead that we are loss.

Love is one energy system that contains all that is. There is nothing that lies outside of it. The nature of love is extension. Because it knows itself to be love it seeks to extend itself, to give of itself. Knowing itself completely, it knows eternal peace. This peace is a deep, profound appreciation of what is. From this peace, of knowing and loving without reserve comes the ability to open oneself entirely to the love which you believe is outside of you. From this opening comes Joy. Joy is not stillness; it is exuberance which cannot be contained. It must be shouted from the rooftops. It is a gift truly received, one that cannot be denied, that must be given to be known completely. To know yourself, you must know giving and receiving as one act of merging with the divine. Peace is the perfect balance of love without question, Joy is imbalance without fear. This is the nature of growth, a cycle of balance and imbalance. Joy is the knowing that giving does not involve loss. Giving love increases love, here lies the balance of the divine.

We have forgotten this is so. We do not know the true nature of love. We think that love is loss. That is what we see in this world. Everything you love will one day be lost, turned to dust. If you know the world only through perception, this is all you can ever know. We must escape perception to escape loss.

The greater our identification with the ego, the greater our denial of our true power. The ego is a victim, that *is* its identity. It is not responsible for the things that happen to it. Everything is someone else's fault. It does not believe it has the power to effect change and so it rails against reality. In Truth our thoughts are of the joyful extension of love through creation, but here we have robbed our thoughts of the ability to create. Thus our thoughts take on the qualities ascribed to them by the ego. As a powerless victim our thoughts are logically fearful. We are adrift in a swirling sea of chaos, death and destruction around every bend. If you doubt this, read the newspaper or watch the news on TV, they will assure you that this is so.

Because we confuse the nature of love, we divide what is one, the energy of consciousness, into two discernible, and we believe, controllable parts. We separate love into the acts of giving and receiving. We believe peace is the passive act of reception and joy the action of giving. We mistake both the separation of the two and the nature of giving and receiving. We believe it is possible to experience one without the other. When we allow ourselves to experience a small degree of love we attempt to exert control over it by maintaining this division. We think this will protect us from loss. When we deny love, we deny ourselves and lock our self in a state of perpetual shame. Shame is the absence of love, so in a sense it is a negative state of being in that it is without love. In order to block out love we divide shame into anger and fear. Anger ensures that we cannot know peace, fear that we cannot know joy, at least not for any extended length of time. If we allow these emotions to reside in our subconscious, love cannot live in our heart.

As we divide love so too do we divide thought from emotion. To thought we give only passive energy and say they are of little consequence. To emotion we give active energy and thus our emotions decide the state of our being and determine the course of our lives. This is a false separation. In truth our thoughts and emotions are one. In thought lies creation, it is the source of extension. By dividing it from the active energy of emotion we leave it virtually powerless. We believe our only means of creation is through form. Our hands must build the ideas of our mind. When we are truly joyful, we must express ourselves. We insist that our emotions find form. This unity of thought and emotion is truth. Thought holds the power of creation, emotion the constancy of being. Yet we rarely know joy, and we allow our thoughts to be controlled by ego.

In Truth, Love is all powerful, nothing can be denied it. Nothing but good could ever be asked of it. We do not believe this. As pure consciousness what we believe, is. We place our focus on the ego which says that all power is outside of self. Thus we give away our power. We do not believe we have the power to create without physically manipulating external objects. A sculpture can exist within one's mind but does not take form without hands and chisel to shape the marble. Everything on our planet not produced by the earth's natural systems, existed as an idea first. In someone's mind first existed the chair I am sitting in, the blanket that covers me, the lamp that provides light and the pen I am writing with, all ideas first. Because we do not believe in the infinite power of our mind there must be an intervening process by which our physical being turns idea into "reality". We manipulate externals to produce things we desire. We place our own internal power outside of ourselves.

Anger

Anger, the active element of shame, looks only at the past. If you are angry it is because what is happening to you now is being evaluated according to the parameters that were set in your childhood. If you came to believe that it was unacceptable for someone to speak to you in a certain manner then every time someone does so you will become angry. For anger to lose its hold on you, you must learn to give up the ideas you acquired in the past.

You must cease to judge the past so that you may cease to judge the present. This releasing of the past allows you to experience peace.

Anger wishes to assert itself over others. It places itself in a superior position and seeks to denigrate the other. It feels it is right and fully justified in all of its actions. Its response is solely because of the actions of the other. Anger wishes only to destroy and that is what it does, every time.

You may continue to delude yourself into thinking that anger is not a choice that you make, thus giving yourself permission to behave as you will. But it is your choice and the choice you make is far greater than you realize. Regardless of your awareness of it, you share yourself with others. When you interact with another you bring to them your energy. They can feel yours, you can feel theirs. When you have an exchange with someone that is lighthearted you walk away feeling better than before you met up with them. When you have an exchange that is tense or angry, you walk away feeling worse for the interaction. Your energy level varies according to the exchange and the degree to which you are connected to spirit.

You have many choices when it comes to dealing with other people. First, will you seek out or will you avoid people who live in an angry world? You will make this decision unconsciously, as we all do. You will be with people who are like you. If you are angry, you will be with angry people. If you are peaceful, you will be with peaceful people. It is not yet possible in our world to live among the general population and avoid angry people altogether. They will be at your workplace, on the road and, if you have teenagers, in your home. When you encounter them, you will have a choice to make, to what extent, if at all, will you allow them to separate you from the energy of love. You will also decide to what extent you will further disconnect or reconnect your adversary to love. You do not make decisions for others, but you do decide what you will share with them. That you *will* share with them is not a choice. Your choice will fall somewhere between the peace of love and the anger of shame. You will lean towards love or shy away from it.

Anger is a child's emotion. It is the nature of the ego which believes the world should conform to its desires. Finding that it does not do so, it attempts to insist that all behave according to its whims. As you mature emotionally, which is the same as spiritually, you begin to give up childish ideas that leave you at the mercy of uncontrollable emotion. You do not suppress anger; you deal with it at its source. You look back to where anger began for you. You begin to recognize the triggers that continue to affect you. As you plumb your emotional past you find the source of the anger and then you look beneath it. Always beneath the anger is fear and pain, pain you did not wish to experience. In pain you feel acutely the absence of the energy of love, like a desert cactus dependent on the blazing sun suddenly put into a dark closet and left to die. This is the experience of pain. Pain which is judgment against the events of the moment leaves you powerless, a victim of another or of circumstance, disconnected from love.

That we experience unfair or even abusive treatment as children is an unfortunate fact at our current level of spiritual evolution. That we pass laws and create agencies to try and prevent it means we are heading in the right direction. The question is, how long do you wish to make your life about your past? Whatever terrible things may be there, if you do not forgive them, or cease to judge them, they remain a part of you. You will continue to hold the anger you feel protects you. You will continue to see anger as strength and ignore the fact that it destroys everything it touches. You will remain disconnected from self, the most painful state a human being can endure. You have to deal with the pain and you have to let it go.

The decision to work through a painful past is not an easy one. It will require you to face what you have denied and you will have to look through the fear you have placed around the memory. We are all tired of carrying our burdens; it is time for us to let them go. It is time for us to live in truth. We are a people who have allowed themselves identity through self-deception. There are many therapists, counselors, psychologists and psychiatrists who can help you work through a painful past. You can find a good one and see them with the conviction of personal honesty. Therapy is not meant to be easy. You will have to experience fully what you have tried to deny, and thus held on to. When you are done you will be able to let it go. You will be able to remove your judgment from the event, or from the person. You are not done until anger is gone from your heart. It may be momentarily experienced in day-to-day life, because other angry people will want to share their anger with you, but having nothing to attach it to from the past, it will come and go. You will recognize in another, the person you once were, and you will not judge. It is essential in spiritual growth to forgive your past. Your past IS your personal truth. Nothing new can ever happen to you until you begin to let this go. Everything will be run through the same filters and thought processes the ego established long ago.

Fear

Beneath anger, always there is fear. If your past was not as you wanted it to be, then how can the future hold anything different? You must be willing to forgive the past before you can forgive the future. Forgiveness means letting go of judgment. It is fear of what is to come that keeps us from experiencing sustained Joy. This fear may simply be that the future will not hold perfection, as in, I will have to do laundry tomorrow and I don't like laundry. Or it may be a more pronounced and incapacitating fear that tragedy will strike out of nowhere or the events that are currently unfolding will end badly. Fear is a passive or inactive state because it renders us incapable of being in the moment but locks our focus on what is to come. The more we allow fear to dominate our thought processes the less able we are to make good decisions that would result in what we would see as a positive outcome.

Fear feeds upon itself, as does anger. When you experience fear, you believe that you are vulnerable to circumstances, thus you are removed from the peaceful energy of love. This causes more fear and can lead to a desperate cycle of depression. Have you ever noticed when you begin to be fearful you find more and more things to be afraid of?

Energetically, if you live with the thought of fear, you

will draw to yourself fearful things. They may not be circumstances or events that you imagine but you will find yourself surrounded by people who experience themselves in a similar way. They are like you and so you are more comfortable with them than others. If you surround yourself with people who live completely without joy, you and they together will manifest fearful things. You will find in your circumstances that there is good reason to be afraid. Your focus will fall upon only the frightening, never the comforting. If someone tries to provide you with comfort, you will tell them why they should be afraid.

It is especially difficult for us to give up fear because it is what we believe keeps us safe. We believe being afraid is good; it keeps us from walking out onto a busy highway or making some other foolish decision that will result in injury or death. Fear of emotional injury keeps us from just giving our heart away to anyone. We believe our bodies physiological response to fear allows us to run faster or fight harder. We think fear protects us.

In fear lives the need to defend. Fear implies vulnerability to some form of attack. Thus one must defend oneself in order not to succumb to the attacker. Here is anger born. Anger is fear externalized and placed upon another, the one who is to blame for your fear. In order to no longer be fearful the "other" must be destroyed. That the "other" undoubtedly feels the same way about you is irrelevant, Fear attacks fear and feeds upon itself. The fearful are only comfortable around the fearful. They will give you plenty of reasons to be afraid. They will brand you weak and foolish if you refuse to agree. They want you to feel as they do, they want to block your connection to peace because they find it threatening to their sense of self. They do not know any other way and believe that giving up fear means their destruction. Darkness is destroyed by the light but is replaced with Truth...with Joy.

The world is more than happy to highlight for us the reasons to be fearful. There are endless sources of fear. You are told repeatedly that you are vulnerable; you will receive this message until you no longer agree to listen. You will be told that anything you have you could lose. The economy could collapse, you could lose your job, your home, your spouse, loved ones...you could get cancer. You or a loved one could be in a terrible accident. When I was in elementary school they told us to be afraid there might be another ice age. Now they tell us to be afraid of global warming.

Fear extends itself through power. If you have power it must be over something or someone. At the root of power is always fear. There is no need for you to have power over that which does not frighten you. Power implies loss. That which it is over could conceivably rise up and take the power away or it could simply cease to exist.

One Energy System

We are one energy system; as such we are interconnected at an energetic, unconscious level. Because we operate from a belief in loss, we believe that for us to gain another must lose. It is as if we say there is only so much emotional energy on the earth. In order to feel good, I must have as much of it as possible. We do not even begin to realize that the energy we seek is of loss. Again, we look in the wrong place, outside of ourselves for what we need. In order for me to have more energy, you must have less. In order for me to be powerful, I must have power over something. There must be someone who has less power for me to be powerful. Your loss is inherent in my gain. The rich and powerful could not exist without the poor and middle class. The boss could not be without the employees.

This belief in gain and loss exists throughout the system. It is inherent in most interpersonal interaction. If you perceive that someone is verbally attacking you, you react as if they were taking something away from you. You essentially grant them power over you by allowing their words to lessen your sense of self. You immediately react by trying to take something back from them. You might return the verbal assault in kind. You might "take the high road" and walk away, then talk about them behind their back. You might internalize the event and spend more of your precious energy trying to rationalize the injury away.

It is a rare individual who is so complete unto themselves that they do not allow others to take from them. They recognize in others the same motivation and desires we all have. In Truth one human being can take nothing from another. They can only participate in events that may encourage another to believe they have lost something. The problem, again, is the belief in loss.

When we separate ourselves from universal love, when we deny our own identity, we create within ourselves a negative energy system. We are essentially empty. We seek a restoration of balance. If we identify ourselves totally with the ego we believe that the only way to gain is by another's loss. We must take something from them and we believe they will attempt to take something from us. We believe anger can defend us from loss and that it has the ability to take power away from others. We can "put them in their place." Of course, the truth is that anger can only destroy.

Energy Balance

Because the balance in our world still tips towards negative, it is easier for negative energy to spread. It is easy enough to watch this happen. Observe human behavior and determine for yourself if this is so. Watch as one angry person gives their anger to another, who then passes it along. At its source it is strongest and dilutes as it is passed, unless it finds itself another source. That it is likely to find another source is no accident. Ask yourself this question, having just been berated by your boss, do you seek out a person who will point out that the boss's wife just left him and maybe you shouldn't have missed an important deadline or do you seek out the person who will tell you what a jerk the boss is and you should file a grievance against him? Like attracts like. This is so at a vibrational level, this is so at a visible tangible level. Think of the angry people in your life, are they not always looking for a reason to be angry? Seizing upon the latest political events, railing at the personal slights they feel are forever being handed them? They are operating at a negative energy level, they are operating without true self. It is a painful state of being, one they try desperately to escape by putting it off onto someone else. The fact that this only increases their pain is lost upon them. Anger lashes out in attack. Anger must give of itself, just as love must. The difference, of course, is that anger destroys its host and seeks to destroy the recipient.

We think this is the nature of love as well. We cannot grasp that in a positive energy system, loss is impossible. To give love benefits both giver and receiver equally, there is no loss.

The Body

As conscious energy we manifest ourselves in a form consistent with our beliefs. We become a body, vulnerable to innumerable attackers from outside itself, viruses, germs, injury, carcinogens, pollution. We are also vulnerable to attackers from within, aging, cancer. Yet this body we envision cannot escape truth entirely though we envision ourselves separate we are wholly and entirely dependent on what is outside of ourselves.

We believe we are a separate entity and so we manifest a body encased in flesh which serves as a distinct boundary between what is ourselves and what we judge is not. Yet the body is completely and utterly dependent on what lies outside of it. As a body we are an energy system with limited resources. We deplete our resources with daily activity, regardless of whether we lead an active or sedentary life. Because we believe in separation, we must physically acquire energy from a tangible outside source, we must eat. We ingest calories, energy, to sustain our bodily process that allows for physical activity. From food we acquire energy for action. The beauty of our physical form lies in its inability to escape Truth. We are beings of energy, the only true energy is love, thus the more energy we expend the more we acquire. The more we exercise the more energy reserves we acquire. This is counterintuitive in a world of loss, yet makes perfect sense if you view the energy of our system as Love without loss. Love given is love extended, here there is only increase. It is the same with the active energy of our body, the more we use, the more we receive, whether we choose to give of it as we are meant to determines its nature.

Active energy will be expressed. It will be given in love or it will be given in shame. The more limited the focus of your consciousness, the more you identify with ego and preference, the greater your need to place yourself above others and thus the greater need to express yourself with anger. When you live at the energetic level of anger, you believe only in active energy. You believe that there is active energy within you and active energy outside of you. For one to gain the other must lose. It is a constant battle between what is within and what is without, though they are one and the same. Anger attracts anger, and from there the battle ensues. The ego says I must be special; I must be different from others in order to have an identity. Thus it is threatened the most by people who are like it. From energy standpoint it must vibrate at a different frequency thus it seeks to lower those around it. It feels it is justified in putting people in their place. Anger lashes out most aggressively at those who are the most like it.

Passive energy is what, in separation, we perceive to be the core of our being. It is who and what we think we are. As such, it is a system, we believe is ours alone. We do not feel compelled to share to share our deepest thoughts with anyone. Yet passive energy must be replenished from outside as well, we must sleep. When we sleep we leave ourselves completely and utterly vulnerable to our environment. We may lock ourselves in our house, set alarms and smoke detectors, but so long as we are sleeping we will not be able to protect ourselves. We cannot escape this requirement of our body. Our brain must have sleep in order to replenish chemicals necessary for thought. If we do not sleep our ability to process information will be negatively impacted.

When you live at the energetic level of fear, you believe that active energy is outside of you and only passive energy within. Thus you perceive yourself to be constantly under attack from your environment. You do not believe that you have within yourself the ability to handle external situations. You have given all of your power to what is outside of you. In interpersonal relationships, fear is most threatened by people it perceives to be superior. They feel diminished by those they do not feel they compare well to. They are afraid their weaknesses will be highlighted by the other. Thus fear also seeks to bring the other down, to lower the others energy. Fear makes insulting comments, either to someone's face or behind their back. It believes that both of these methods are effective in knocking the other down a peg of two.

When you are able to move past fear to peace, you no longer see the external world as threatening. Your consciousness has separated itself from fearful thoughts and no longer sees the ego's world. It sees what is within it as also outside of it. Peace accepts itself and thus it is able to accept others. Yet peace we see as passive energy, one that reflects itself but does not reshape or change.

Peace

Peace is a greater state of knowing oneself. It is a feeling of profound and unquestioning appreciation of what is. Because we do not know ourselves we do not know peace, the quiet place where creation stirs. Peace comes in the release of the past. In releasing the past from judgment we let go of anger. We let go of one barrier between ourselves and Love. We change what we give to those around us. In our state of personal peace, we cannot help but share peace with others. It is a fundamental shift in the state of our soul. You will no longer experience anger and its shadows of frustration and discontent. In peace you have come to accept one aspect of your true self, you are safe, wholly and completely, always and forever safe. Thus you have also given up fear. You now totally accept what is outside of yourself, you no longer judge. A state of perfect peace requires the relinquishment of judgment entirely.

This is how our physical incarnation reflects our true being. We must rest and so to must we be active. Our physical survival depends upon us achieving a reasonable balance between the two, just as our spiritual growth depends upon us finding the balance between energy systems. You cannot have one without the other without being decidedly unbalanced. We take in energy from outside ourselves thru eating and sleeping. Eating gives us the energy for action which corresponds to the subconscious and emotion. Sleep restores our energy for thought which corresponds to passive energy. Even in our separated state we must maintain some balance between the two in order to survive in our physical body, thus we have one physical need that supersedes all others, we must breathe.

In breath lies balance. It is an automatic action our body takes to survive. A deep, slow deliberate breathe serves to calm both our thought and emotion. Not only does it center us within ourselves it can be a constant reminder that we are dependent upon the unseen energy which is all around us. We like to believe we are separate, it is not so. Our body is not a self-sustaining energy system, it requires energy from outside sources and so we must take in what is outside of us, process it within our body, expel it so it can be used again by the greater system. We are an integral part of the whole, regardless of our willingness to accept this.

Joy

The active energy of love is Joy. The active energy of shame is fear. Fear is the absence of Joy, not its opposite. To call it opposite would be to imply that it is real, it is not, is simply the absence of what is real. However, where one is experienced, the other cannot be. In Joy you know yourself wholly and completely. Whereas peace is the acceptance of what is outside of you, Joy is the acceptance of what is within. It is the removal of judgment from self. You are willing to accept yourself as love entirely. With the acceptance of Joy you are now able to give and receive fully. In Truth the two become one, you become a part of the energetic flow of all that is. What you receive is inherently given, because that is what you are. There is no longer need to be angry, you are not afraid. There is no longer need to withhold, you are safe. No longer must you deny yourself, you are Love. It is the allowing of yourself to receive that allows the energy of creation to flow through you and the peace of God's love to settle upon you.

As a single point of focus, I am powerless. All of the energy of consciousness is outside of my awareness. So long as my focus remains narrow, I remain a closed system. Energy will move through me because I must be what I am, but it will carry with it the energy of loss. As a narrow point, I attempt to keep the energy within me, separate from the energy without. Energy contained becomes stagnate, it is love unexpressed. Love unexpressed becomes fear; fear that all of the true power is outside of you and that as a separate entity you could only be its victim.

The victim becomes angry, enraged over its diminished state. It attempts to assert itself to its rightful position through the energy of loss. Anger can never achieve this. The victim must learn what it truly is. We think we hold on to things because we don't have enough when in fact it is the very act of holding on that keeps us from receiving everything. We hold ourselves separate from the abundance of the universe.

The subconscious is an emotional block between our focus and our being or spirit. It is a barrier that our ego feeds to keep us from recognizing truth. The thought of fear blocks the emotion of Joy. The emotion of anger blocks our thoughts of peace. Peace comes to us when we are willing to let go of the past. When we relinquish the past from preference we experience peace. For most of us there are things about our past that we do not like, things we wish had not happened or had happened differently. In some instances our entire being becomes centered on one tragic event. We experience anger or pain in relationship to these memories, thus we hold on to a moment which has long since passed.

Fear is of the future, for the events which are yet to come. We do not experience Joy because we are afraid we may not be able to handle what is ahead. Fear is truly the fear of self, our own inability to deal with the future. This is why the experience of Joy is only possible when one fully accepts oneself. It is the release of self from preference, knowing that whatever happens things are always ok. We experience limited amounts of joy because we refuse to relinquish the future from preference.

In separation we divide love into its passive and active qualities, peace and joy. In truth love cannot be divided and so any attempt to sustain one without the other is temporary. If we hope to achieve joy, we must first find peace. If we hope to maintain peace we must find joy. The Truth of our being is Love united as one. If we let go of the past (anger) we know peace, if we let go of the future (fear) we know Joy. Without past and future, we are within the moment, the only moment which has ever been.

Health

Depending on the balance of our thoughts and emotions, energy will become blocked at certain points in our body and become illness or injury. Our body is entirely a manifestation of our emotional state of being. A person who lives completely in the absence of authentic creation lives a life of emptiness. It is our nature to create, to use the power of our mind to make something where before there was nothing. True creation comes from our emotional center. It reflects either love or its absence. It is love made manifest. It is unnatural for us not to extend ourselves through creation.

Giving vs. Receiving

We mistake, or reverse, in perception the true energetic nature of giving and receiving. We see giving as active and receiving as passive. In fact, it is easier to give love than it is to receive it though this is counterintuitive. To give love you do not need to open yourself. To truly receive love it must be done without judgment. To receive love without judgment is to connect yourself to universal consciousness. In order to do this you must forgive the past and let go of all old anger. You must let go of all fear so that you no longer hold yourself separate. You drop all boundaries, opening yourself to something you perceive of as outside of yourself. This is the act of surrender and there is no greater action, no greater gift a human being can give.

It is the receiving of love that gives you joy. It is giving love that brings you peace. In truth there is no separation, as you breathe in, so to must you breathe out. You are one with creation. Because we misunderstand the nature of giving and receiving, peace which is passive involves the giving up of anger which is active. Joy which we see as active means relinquishing fear which is passive. The truth of course lies in the perfect balance of peace and joy, which is love given and received in equal measure. There is no need to hold on to anything because love is all there is. You are free, entirely open to everything that is, that has ever been and may one day be, because in all of these places you will know only love.

"In Love"

When you are "in love", what you would call romantic love, what you experience is the balance of giving and receiving. You drop your boundaries for that one "special" person so that for that brief magical time you are willing to give and receive in kind. What you feel, for that one special person, is an openness that allows you to experience universal love…to a very small, very controlled degree. You limit the universal to one individual who for a brief period of time is deemed an acceptable recipient of your deepest self. Everything looks better when you are in love. People you could not stand before are somehow more tolerable now, the sky is bluer, the grass greener. But you have placed tight restrictions on this love; it must behave within a narrow set of parameters. As with all things, he/she must behave in the way you expect them to. Their actions must not brush up against anything from your unforgiven past. If it does, you will likely judge this as an intentional attempt to hurt you. You will feel the need to defend yourself, you will become angry. Your anger will likely trigger a similar response in your beloved. The barriers you had dropped are now firmly restored. You may stay with this person, you may still love them but you are no longer in perfect balance with them. Now when you give you expect it to be returned in a certain way, you place judgment upon it. When you receive you measure its value, you no longer let it flow through you with Joy.

Interaction

We act upon each other as if we were individual magnets operating within a larger magnetic field. The larger field contains all of us who chose to live and learn as human beings. We, as individuals, exist somewhere along the spectrum of absolute negative energy (no connection to spirit) to absolute positive (knowing we are only spirit). Those at either end of the spectrum are the most rare, most fortunate in the case of the negative and most unfortunate at the other end. For most of us, we are somewhere in the middle, with moments of lower energy and moments of higher. If we live a life of personal honesty, we grow spiritually as we grow emotionally and end our life at a higher point than we began.

As we move through this existence we interact with many others, some with whom we will have close relationships and others with whom we will briefly share the same space. Yet with each and every person you encounter there is an interaction, a shift in the energy field created by proximity. Depending upon the nature of the field and your own connection to spirit, you may be gently or forcefully pulled in one direction. You may go shopping and within the store encounter a number of people you perceive to be rude. Have you ever noticed that where there is one, there tend to be more? The energy of the environment affects everyone in it. Once someone has been rude to you, you are likely to be angry and irritated.

You carry that energy with you to your next interaction. You may or may not be rude but your vibrational energy has likely dropped a notch or two, and you will now share this with those around you. Whether you think of this from an energy standpoint or not, the environment you inhabit has a tremendous impact on your emotional state. If you come home one day and everyone there is in a good mood (even if you are not) the odds are that your mood will improve, pulled up by the miracle which has occurred within your home. On the other hand you may have had the best day ever but if you come home to find World War III erupting in your living room, you would have to be a highly evolved individual to not allow this to bring you down.

The importance here is to recognize the impact you have on other human beings. If you share a space, even briefly, there is at least a gentle push or pull. If as you pass someone you look at them, say hello and smile, there will be a gentle pull. If instead you keep your head down and do not speak, there is a gentle push. You have pretended as if the person who just passed was not there. The more time you spend with someone the greater your influence upon them, and theirs on you.

My magnet science may be a bit off, but for the moment we are going to pretend that magnets work the way I want them to. Opposites do not attract. Negative attracts negative, positive attracts positive. You pull to you, like a magnet, those individuals and events that match your energy level. It is a pull that you do not recognize and it brings to you things that you did not know were there. You will find yourself dating the same type of person over and over again. You will break up with one and think you will never do that again only to find a few months into your next relationship that the person you at first thought was so different from the others, is in fact just the same. Until you are honest with yourself as to why you attract these people you will continue to do so. You will repeat patterns until you understand the true nature of the repetition.

You will share your energy with those around you. As a single energy system the human race is truly one. You will have the greatest impact on those you chose to share the same space with. For every human being you encounter you will be at least a gentle push or pull. You will push them away from love or pull them towards it. You and they may have no conscious awareness of this, and the effect may be only momentary, not to mention tempered by others in the vicinity, but you always share your energy with those around you. You more likely think of this in terms of mood. People in a distinctly good or bad mood, clearly share their energy (or mood) with everyone around them.

When operating at the energetic level of fear and anger we reject most of the world. It is as if we say, I am only my right little toe, that is all I am willing to be. What could anyone possibly expect of me, I am only this little toe. A toe can only sit and wish it had a foot so that it might get out on occasion. We deny the totality of our being and render ourselves powerless. We are ego only. We are the absence of positive energy; we are closed to the energy of the universe. The more of this world we embrace and accept the larger our energy source. We are open to all that is. We find the emotional balance in ourselves that blends peace and joy into perfect Love.

You have a far greater connection to others than you can likely imagine, yet you are only responsible for yourself. You may encourage others to do well or to fail but ultimately what happens to them is their decision. The best thing you can do to help others, is to first help yourself. To know yourself truly, means you will first exist in a state of peace and ultimately Joy. There is no greater gift you could give to humanity than to exist in this state. As such you will act as a powerful pull towards Love. Others will see in you what is possible for themselves. For some it will be a painful vision. In you they will see loss rather than gain. They will see what they do not have rather than that they are truly the same as you.

Enlightenment is the natural state of humanity. No longer is it only for those who isolate themselves from others and devote their lives to its pursuit. As enlightened beings we are one within ourselves, one within each other and one within God. We are an energy system within a larger energy system. As the smaller system we are completely dependent upon the larger. The larger system is how I have come to see God. He/She/It is everything. God is consciousness undivided; as such the energy of his system is Love. From Joy he gives of himself to expand creation. From Love he allows for his creation to find its own way, to discover themselves and be out of choice, rather than command. In peace he waits for us knowing we will make our way home.

Chapter 10

THE PATH

We are not alone. There is a guiding force which shapes our world. We were not simply unleashed into the vacuum of space and expected to make our way home on our own. The hand of God reaches gently into our dreams and beckons us follow. It points out for us, always, a simple path to our Father's door. It is there for us whenever we choose to take it. We can ignore it for as long as we like but from our rejection will come the lessons we must learn in order to see it clearly. You cannot escape the Truth of what you are, try though you might.

For each of us there is a part we must play in the uniting of our consciousness. Ultimately we will return to our original state. We will be of one mind, one within ourselves, one as humanity and one with God. Until we are ready, we may play many roles, each preparing us to finally choose the path that has been set for us to follow. Here is both free will and destiny combined. You are free to choose against your destiny for as long as you like. Ultimately you must take your place as a part of the whole, but you are free to pretend that you are a separate entity. You can live life after life of empty selfish pursuits, wondering why all your riches are never quite enough. You can convince yourself that love is for fools, that power and control are the only things that can keep you safe. You will search for safety in elements outside yourself, a place where safety cannot be found. You will always know there is something missing, something you just can't quite seem to define. Life will provide the answer for you, as soon as you are willing to know.

Your life is your own, your choices shape its being but the events you experience are in no way random occurrences. We are driven to learn what we are. This is the ultimate question humanity has always faced. Who are we and why are we here? You will seek to answer this question as an individual just as scientists, philosophers and theologians will seek to answer it for us all. You will not rest until you have found your answer. Within a lifetime we call this identity. As you move from child to teen to adult, you must acquire some sense of self. You may spend a large portion of your life looking outside of yourself for this, with any luck, at some point you will begin to look within. Each time you ask for greater understanding an answer will be given to you. You will meet someone and have a discussion that just happens to be on the topic of your question, you will pick up a book and find your question discussed, you will flip past a television show and a few key words will catch your attention...they will catch your focus. You will face tragedy, from this you will either grow or be destroyed. In destruction you will begin again. When you insist on greater understanding, your focus will find an answer. You may not accept the answer the first time it is given, but if you ask with an open mind, eventually you will understand.

Life brings to you the lessons you need to learn. You will keep running up against the same self-imposed boundaries until you learn to overcome them. We work together on this project of unification. We fit together as puzzle pieces. The right teacher will be there to show you what you must learn and you will be there to teach your lessons to those who do not yet understand them. Ultimately what you will come to understand is that you are, and always have been, the master of your fate.

It can be a long journey to understanding. You may spend countless lifetimes working to master a single lesson. Life will unceasingly provide you with the material to learn. Those things that make you angry will emerge repeatedly until you learn that anger's only true quality is destruction. When a change comes it will be made within yourself. Should you doubt the care with which your lessons have been presented think back on your life. Those times that you felt you were most challenged, those events you wished had not occurred, did they not contribute to you learning more about yourself? Some of these lessons can be quite painful and you may question what you believe to be a vengeful God. How could something like this happen? Why do bad things happen to good people? They happen because everyone has lessons to learn. All things work towards ultimate good, of this, there is no question. It is our stubborn refusal to accept our true selves that causes suffering.

Not only will your external choices shape your life, but your internal vibrational choices as well. If you are angry, you will live in an angry world. If you are afraid, you will live in a world full of fearful things. This is a matter of focus, choice and the energy running behind them. You will draw to yourself people and circumstances that are like you. Essentially, the universe will give you what you want, what you truly want. In Truth you can only experience what you believe you are because that is all you will be able to accept. You can only experience what you believe to be true. Your mind will explain away that which you are unprepared to accept. If you do not believe someone loves you, you will rationalize any kindness they may show. Should you be confronted by a miracle of epic proportions, as in the parting of the Red Sea, you will find an explanation that suits your level of understanding.

Nothing is required of you but that you be as you are. One day you will be ready to stop pretending you are something you are not. It is only the path of denial which brings pain. When you deny your true self, you deny your connection to God and you live in absence of his Love. You live without the true energy of self and so you experience pain and suffering. All suffering is a choice we make in opposition to Truth. We can make this choice as long as we wish but so long as we make it, we will suffer.

This is not punishment, it is not Karma. God does not judge us for our decisions; his Love is all that is. To believe God could withdraw his love is to distort the True nature of being. He could no more withdraw his Love from us than we could cease to question the nature of things. It is only we who can pretend to remove our self from Love.

When you are ready to follow the path to Truth, you will find it has been laid out for you. God does not judge, he does not send tragedy to punish you for your misdeeds, but he does send a guiding hand to shape the events of your choosing so that you might learn from them and be spared future pain.

It is the vibrational energy of our being that brings us the lessons we must learn. What you put out into the world is what you bring back to you. You surround yourself with what you believe you are. If you change what you believe to be true of self, then your circumstances will change and you will draw different things into your life. If we are angry we will draw to ourselves angry people and angry events, as well as a state of health shaped by anger. We draw these things to us so that we can see anger for what it is. We can observe the effects it has on others while steadily denying that we ourselves are angry. Eventually we will recognize that what we see and criticize in others, resides within our self.

We draw to us lessons on the level at which we can learn. This does not rule out the great leap of faith. It is possible, though rare, for individuals to take giant spiritual strides, but it requires a truly open heart, if only for an instant. If we are not ready to learn, the physical appearance of God himself could not teach us. We would simply be afraid of that which we did not understand, a most enduring human trait. Fear drives one farther away from Truth and is the most destructive thought in human awareness. You will always be in the right place, at the right time, to see, hear and experience the things that you need to learn. But ultimately it is your choice whether or not to pay attention, it is your choice to learn.

If you look back on your life, however much there has been of it, with the belief that its purpose was to help you remember your true self; do the memories change their hue? Is it the easy times in life or the difficult that helped you to grow? The more painful the event the deeper within you had to reach to survive. Sometimes you learn far more about self from when life says no than from when it says yes. You are meant to do more than survive, you are meant to have it all, to know no limits, no boundaries, but you do not believe this. So long as you do not believe, it cannot be. You will continue to face obstacles until you no longer see them. You believe obstacles are solid, immovable objects, but they are only a means to an end. There are no random events in our lives, we make a choice and life forms itself to support our chance to learn from that choice. You will be drawn to that person at your new job who can show you more about who you are. You will find that this job is not right for you. You will quit your job and later realize that it was the perfect job for you and you quit for a totally egotistical and meaningless reason. From all of this you will learn and when you are ready, opportunity will come to you again. We all know that we learn from mistakes but that leaves us no more willing to make them.

There are terribly painful events that occur in people's lives and I do not make light of their suffering. Yet is it better to see tragedy as a random occurrence or the punishment of a "loving" God? Does it lesson the pain of losing a child to believe that accidents or illness just happen? Or that some fault of your own brought about this karmic retribution?

If you see life as the extension of Love than you can know no loss. What has life cannot cease to be, it can only shift out of our perceptual awareness. It can never leave our true awareness. A part of the whole cannot be lost. The greatest challenges require the greatest growth.

If you believe that life is a series of random occurrences, than all you can be is a victim. You need not take responsibility for anything. You can say, I may have been going 100mph in a 35 mph zone but if there hadn't been a police officer there I would not have gotten a ticket. This leaves you in a state of powerlessness, where you can only be frightened by what may come. This is the ego's fear, where you have no ability to affect events and no responsibility for outcome. If you live a life centered in truth, you acknowledge that to regularly drive over the speed limit means you are likely to receive speeding tickets. To become angry or place blame elsewhere is absurd.

A speeding ticket is a simple scenario, what of the case of a fatal car accident where one driver is clearly responsible for the death of the other? Let's say the driver who caused the accident was drunk and in fact had multiple DUI convictions. The driver who was killed was a young, beloved kindergarten teacher who had three young children of her own and a husband in the military stationed overseas. The ego will call for vengeance, it must place blame and it demands retribution. It will rage at the injustice. The family of the deceased may choose to carry this anger with them for the rest of their lives.

They may hope that the guilty suffers, that somehow the suffering of this other human being can make up for what they have done.

There is no truth in this. Suffering is loss; there is never gain in it. The choice to suffer forever the loss of a loved one is the choice to deny truth. It does not bring the loved one back; it does not somehow make right what was judged wrong. The desire to see others suffer is a terribly heavy burden to carry.

The driver responsible for the accident will suffer. He has made a decision that has resulted in loss; he will have to find truth in order to lay his burden down. He will likely begin with the ego's reasoning. He will see the accident as someone else's fault. The bartender who kept serving him or even the woman who was killed, perhaps he can make himself believe it was her fault. This is not truth and it has no power to ease pain. Only by moving past the ego can one move past a tragic event. He will have to accept that he was responsible for the woman's death, he will have to know it in his heart and then he will have to decide if he is willing to let it go. He will make a choice between being of value or believing he has none. This is where he began. As he sat at the bar night after night, he drank because he did not believe his life had value and events brought to him a painful lesson in which he might choose again.

And what of our beloved kindergarten teacher? To see her now as a victim is to place our self yet again in fear's path. There comes a time in every life when the lessons that can be learned have been, or they have been passed on so many times as to be lost. The purpose of this particular life has been exhausted; there is no reason to continue. The people who will be affected by the death will learn and grow from it…if they choose.

This is a chance for all involved to see that the only thing that really matters is Love and that love can only come from forgiveness. To feel love they must forgive themselves. If they can forgive themselves they can forgive others. There is a deep and powerful lesson here for both sides. Do you value pain or do you value love? You will hold on to one or the other, you cannot hold both. A tragedy such as this will bring this to light, if you let it. Life will bring you to places that the ego cannot make sense of. If necessary, it will bring you repeatedly to this place, until you are able to see through it.

Slowly, we work our way away from anger. We find deeper truth; our anger is caused by pain. We would rather blame others and experience anger than accept the truth of our pain. Over time we begin to see that pain can only reside within our self, as such it belongs solely to us. We begin to see that our emotional state is a choice we make. We can focus on positive things in our life and feel happy or negative things and feel sad. We recognize that this is so for all of us, that truly we are all the same. As we no longer blame others we draw them closer to us. We share more of ourselves because we no longer fear the consequences of doing so. We experience peace as fear has been erased. As the master of our emotions there is nothing to fear. We see that what we have always been the most afraid of was our self, our own suffering, our own fear. We know now that we need not suffer, ever.

Finally we free ourselves completely from judgment; we accept all that is as part of our self. We know Joy, we know Love without division. In the end the most difficult thing for us to accept is not that we are flawed, but that we are flawless.

Chapter 11

THOUGHT

We believe Descartes; we believe we are because we think. The problem is we mistake the True nature of thought. Are we all of our thoughts or only the ones we would choose to associate ourselves with? True thought does not require words. You do not need to explain to yourself what you are experiencing. It is because our mind is divided that one level must use language to explain itself to the next. True thought is a merging of the divide; it is focus and awareness in concert.

The words that float around in our head we consider to be our thoughts. That they are jumbled and frequently at odds with one another we have come to accept as normal. The words in our head may or may not reflect some level of Truth, the best they can ever do is to create a True reflection. If the words come from the ego they cannot know Truth, if they come from a deeper level of mind then there will be deeper Truth. The day will come when you will no longer need words to explain things to yourself. You will know without explanation, because you will finally know yourself. True thought is our true self, it is all that we are and it is everything.

When the heart is empty, thoughts become confused. If you live in the absence of love your mind will try and fill the void. The ego will manufacture false emotions to support its ramblings. Instead of allowing you to feel the pain, the ego at its strongest point will tell you that the people in your life are attempting to destroy you. If you don't protect yourself from them, you will be annihilated. The ego will be sure to remind you of all the times in the past that you have been taken advantage of and treated badly. It will tell you that this justifies any type of violent reaction you might have. It will also tell you that it is not your fault. All of those people in your past are to blame for the actions you take today. It will then take the anger it has created inside of you and places it in the form of hate onto the people it holds responsible for your suffering. At the root of anger is the thought, "it should not be this way." What you must see in order to escape this is that the hate resides within you. The ego has created this thought pattern to protect you from pain. The hate the ego rails against truly is not for others, it is for yourself. You hate the state of your being. You hate the emptiness of your heart. You rage at a world that has allowed you to live this way. This is the nature of thought when the ego has its tightest grip. Because anger lives within you, you need the world to behave as you see fit. If it does not, again, you will feel justified in attempting to forcefully make it the way you think it should be. Any thought of causing harm to another living creature is anger externalized to hate. You may believe that these thoughts bring you comfort, even joy. Any thought that is not of love, serves to block love from your heart. This is how the ego survives. It fills your head with angry thoughts so that you will feel anger. So long as you feel anger you cannot know love and thus the ego is locked safely in the prison of your mind.

If the ego cannot manufacture anger, it is willing enough to settle for fear. Fear can come in a myriad of forms and thus can be more difficult to deal with than anger. The thought at the root of fear is "I am vulnerable." Fearful thoughts can be overt. "I am afraid I will get sick, I am afraid my child will die, I am afraid I will be in a car accident." These thoughts may come and go according to circumstances or they may be a constant part of the ego's repertoire. Whereas anger requires action in order to protect oneself, fear insists on inaction. When you are in the grip of fear you do not believe that you have the power to overcome it. That is the nature of fear. You are a victim locked in a vicious cycle created by external circumstances. To escape this cycle you must accept that you are not a victim, within you resides the ability to handle any event that may come your way.

As fear loses its grip it may take on more subtle forms. You may find yourself threatened by people who you believe think they are superior to you. They may indeed believe this or they may not, it does not matter, the result is the same. You feel that you are diminished by their superiority. If you did not determine your worth according to them, you would not care what they thought about you. Any gain these people experience will trigger fearful thoughts in your mind. The ego will tell you how unfair it is that this person got a new car. It will tell you that you are less because they now have more. Fearful thoughts diminish you, they always tell you you have lost something or may lose something and that when you do you will not be able to handle it.

We concede our identity to our thoughts. We believe that what we think is who we are. We tend to allow anger to shape the nature of who we have been and fear to determine who we are now. This is the point that many of us find ourselves at. It is as if we wear a heavy backpack and carry a heavy suitcase with us and say that they are us. In the backpack are all of things that happened to us that we believe should not have happened. We carry them with us and say that they are a part of us. In the suitcase are all of things we believe we must do in order to make everything be OK. Inherent in this belief is the thought that things are not OK as they are. Once I pay off the mortgage, or the credit card, or get this project done, or clean the house then I will feel better. If you knew yourself whole and complete, you would have no need of these burdens you carry. You could shed the backpack and know peace, you could put down the suitcase and know joy.

The problem with determining the nature of thought is that our focus can drift from one level to the next and back again in a matter of minutes, perhaps even seconds. It can even hold multiple levels of thought simultaneously. You can refuse to forgive certain people from your past but chose to forgive others. Thus you will only be angry when you are dealing with these people or with people who you judge to be like them in some way. You will also be angry when the world does not conform to your desires in the way you have determined that it should.

When you do not get your way, at some point you will likely get angry or at least irritated. You can go from being angry one moment to fearful the next. Feeling fearful or vulnerable might then make you mad. Then you might see something beautiful that just for a moment transports you to another place. Then you come right back. The more words that fill your mind, the more your focus is pulled in multiple directions. This is an exhausting state of being. To try and categorize the originating level of mind for every thought would be impossible and pointless for most people. As you settle into a more peaceful state of being, your mind begins to quiet. The ego may still pipe up on occasion and attempt to steal your focus but peace recognizes the egos ploys.

In general you can be certain that thought is dominated by ego if thoughts are of harm coming to other people. This is anger or fear in one of its multiple forms. If you have the desire to hurt someone, this is anger. You can assume that your thoughts originate in fear if they are of harm coming to someone, though not by your hand. If you would really sort of enjoy it if your next door neighbor wrecked that new sports car, this is a fearful thought. You believe you would gain by his loss. When you judge others, this thought comes from ego, peace does not need to judge. When you can accept yourself as you are, you can accept the world as it is. There is greater truth in fear than anger. There is far greater truth in peace than fear, but truth does not lie here either. Truth lies in joy which is the nature of our soul.

You believe there is a difference between thought and emotion, there is not. This is simply a part of the division you have created within your true self. Consider for a moment, a time in your life when you came to understand something wholly and completely, without question. Some would call this an epiphany, but it need not be so dramatic. How did you know that you had come to a new understanding? Was it the words in your mind or the lack of them? Wasn't it the *feeling* of understanding and the accompanying quiet? When you truly know you do not need to use words, true knowing is a feeling. It is a feeling which contains no judgment only complete acceptance. You may very shortly after understanding, begin to describe in words your new found understanding but this is just a habit you acquired long ago. Words can never do justice to true understanding. True knowing comes from spirit. Thus when thought comes from spirit you inherently recognize its Truth, you simply *know*.

At any time in life, thought may come from spirit. In a quiet moment when the ego has momentarily stilled, True thought may enter one's mind. The larger and more dense the layer of the subconscious the more active the ego, the more difficult time spirit has to capture awareness. But spirit has an advantage; it is thought and emotion as one. It knows truth, it does not know doubt. And so in the momentary lapse of the ego, Sprit will speak. It is that deep inner voice that you know is Truth. It will tell you, if you let it, when something you are doing is taking you on a different path than you are meant to take. It will tell you to turn left instead of right. It is your choice to listen or not but both your thoughts and emotions will respond to it.

We are lost in our own mind. Our thoughts are fractured,

originating at competing levels of consciousness. Yet we believe that this is who we are. What we believe is what we experience. If our thoughts are dominated by anger, then we live in a world of anger. If our thoughts are dominated by fear, there is much to be afraid of. We think that the world we see is "real," that what we see is what is. We do not understand that we see the world only through perception which is based entirely on thought. The ego cannot know truth and thus, there is no truth in perception.

Chapter 12

METAPHOR

There is a clear purpose for our existence here. We are not victims of fate, adrift in a sea of chance. We are given this home, our earth, to learn. Here the lessons are inherent in our every experience. Our home is a metaphor for Truth. It is for us to look past the blinders of perception and see the Truth that is within all things. The earth shows us gently what we are meant to understand. It may take lifetimes of gentle persuasion or lifetimes of pain but one day you will see what has always been.

The ego relies on language to explain the world to you. Language creates a barrier between self and experience. A metaphor circumvents language, requiring a deeper level of understanding. It is a puzzle that when put in place is truly known. It creates within your mind a quiet place where Truth may reside. Truth is thus known with True thought, not with the ego's blather. A metaphor is a beautiful expression of Truth presented to us in a way we may understand. Our earth is this expression.

The earth and our experiences here hold all of the answers

to any question we could ever ask. It tells us who we are and where we came from. It shows us the True nature of being and does so at whatever level of Truth we are willing to accept. Within every lifetime there will come a time, if only once, that you will allow the earth to reach out and speak just to you. You will know this in the cessation of breath and the quieting of your mind. You will for an instant experience its beauty. It may come in your first view of the ocean, of the mountains, a field of flowers, a sunset or even a barren desert. It is beauty deeply experienced, it is Truth manifest and at least for an instant you will simply be. The earth speaks at all times; it is only up to you to listen.

Our home shows us what we believe to be true. It shows us separation. We are male and female, not one but two. It shows us the separation of life sustaining elements, fire, water, earth, air. It shows us loss. In nature the destruction of one is required for the sustenance of another. Life here appears to be temporary, ashes to ashes and dust to dust. Existence itself is divided by time. We experience a past, present and future. Life here appears to be the play of opposites. There is right and wrong, good and bad, too much or too little. Yet, life is not lived well in opposition. The earth's first lesson is balance. Life exists in the balance of things.

Our earth sits poised between sun and moon. A little closer to the sun and the planet would be too hot to sustain life, a little farther away and it would be too cold. The moon sits just close enough to regulate the ocean's tides. Life evolved here because there was balance.

All of the earth's systems require balance. Not enough

rain, there is drought; too much rain there is flood. A gentle wind carries seeds to new destinations; hurricane force winds destroy everything in its path. Because we believe in loss, we tend to view life on our planet as a bitter struggle for survival, be that physical or emotional, rather than seeing our home as the provider of all our needs. It has the perfect temperature, the right atmosphere to support our respiration, water to drink, vegetation (and animals if you choose) to eat. Here are the materials to build the stuff of our imagination. We can take what we find here and build space ships, we can manufacture medicines. We can harness electricity to power all manner of gizmos and gadgets. Our planet is perfectly suited to our physical and intellectual needs. We have everything we need and yet we insist it is not enough.

All life must find its balance to survive. A tree must have earth to hold its roots. It must have water in proper measure, too much it will drown or its roots give way. Too little and it will die. It must have the sun's heat in the summer time and the winter's cool to set its spring's fruit. It can survive only within a certain range of conditions. Too far outside of these and it will cease to be. Human life is the same as this tree. We must have enough food to eat and water to drink. We must have the oxygen the tree will provide for us as it must have the carbon dioxide we exhale. We are interdependent, all we creatures that find ourselves here. Our survival is dependent on the survival of others. The earth teaches us that we cannot be one without the other.

Earth without water is barren. Remove one element and our physical existence as humans is at an end. Place one element out of balance with the others and we see the loss caused by imbalance. The earth shows us in all of its systems that in balance there need not be loss.

A flower shows us the beauty of perfect balance. It does not matter that it lasts only a few days. In its essence is the moment. To come into being the plant must have the proper balance of the elements. Too little or too much of any one and the plant will not bloom. It may still live, with the potential to bloom another day, but it will exist in a diminished state much as we do in this place.

Creation

The earth tells us the story of our creation in metaphor, over and over again. It is the same story of our individual birth and humanities birth. We began as one, what we are came from life that was before we gained awareness. Once we were one with the originating consciousness, a seamless whole containing multiple levels of awareness and infinite points of focus. Love extended itself to create us and we were given focus and with it all levels of awareness. In order to use our focus, to know ourselves, we must grow, and so we move from infant, incapable of focus, to adult seeking to know the true nature of self. We must move past adult capable of focusing on falsehoods to Truth.

The story begins in the ocean, the ocean that once covered all of our earth and thus was everything and it begins in the ocean of our mother's womb. There we began as a simple celled organism, dividing, growing becoming more complex. There we grew limbs that we did not need to walk and lungs that we did not need to breath. Here we stayed until we had what we needed to move on, we crawled ashore, pushed from our mother's womb and took a breath, the first breath of separation, no longer supported entirely by our mother yet not abandoned. Our mother would care for us, provide for our needs as we learned to create our own balance. As our bodies grew we learned to focus, we began to understand that we were not our surroundings, we became more complex beings capable of more complex levels of thinking. Over the millennia we grew, living in balance with our mother, moving with her gentle currents, following our food supply, living and dying according to her conditions.

As we grew we came to understand that our hands could change our surroundings. We learned to stack blocks, we learned to sharpen stones. We moved from observing our surroundings to interacting and altering it to suit our needs. Our minds became capable of symbolic thought; we used words or drew pictures on cave walls. We began to care for those who cared for us. We wanted them to be with us, we grieved when they were lost. We wept when our mother left us behind, we sprinkled flowers on the grave of ancient lost loved ones, burying with them those precious items we felt would protect them in the next place. We learned to love but with it we always experienced loss. The physical and cognitive developments we take for granted in the first year of one life, took place over millions of years of human evolution.

We existed in this early time mainly on one level of awareness with the ever increasing ability to hold our own focus. It was a simple and seamless division of mind. Yet, it was division, it was mind which held the belief in separation, and so we chose to learn and grow in separation, but what we will learn is to return to our original state of unity.

As we evolved we learned the nature of separation. Here there is loss, here there is pain, yet even this will ultimately serve the purpose of our growth. We grew to the point that we could cognitively process and experience emotional loss, not simply hunger, cold or physical suffering but a diminished state of emotional being. We collectively moved past learning to focus our consciousness, we mastered the ability to create balance within our being so that we might survive a physical existence. In this mastery we experienced pain, we did not like loss, we did not want it to feel the emptiness and so we sought to deny it. We told ourselves that if we denied it, it need not be so; we began to lie to ourselves. We began to look away from pain as if that would eliminate its existence. We gave our focus away to that which promised to protect us and allowed a lie to settle into the core of our being. Now there was a distinct division of mind, now life was no longer a matter of balance with our caregiver, now the ego had come to tell you, you must be afraid.

For those living in the earliest state of being there was no question of personal identity, the cognitive ability to do so did not yet exist. For an individual living during the Stone Age they knew themselves to be a part of the whole. They were a member of the clan. Their age and gender determined their responsibilities within the clan. Their responsibilities were intrinsic to the survival of the group. They were a part of the whole. Similarly a small child does not question his position in the world. He is a part of his surroundings, whatever they may be. There is a fundamental shift in identity when man begins to alter his relationship with his provider, be it mother or mother earth. Civilization says that some are of more value than others. The Priests, the Kings they are needed but there is a growing portion of society that really is not. Civilization imposes identity. You are a product of your position at birth that is all you are. You have no control over your position regardless of being peasant or priest. Not only do you not have control but you have the cognitive capacity to recognize that this is so.

And so the first age of the ego begins. It comes at the point in evolution when the child shifts its relationship with its caregiver. Now the child knows himself as a separate entity and believes he is no longer reliant on mother earth. He is adrift without anchor. He believes on one level of mind (focus) that this is what he wants but on the other (subconscious), he is a motherless child and he is frightened and angry at his abandonment. Anger will become his shield against pain and fear. When mankind learned to domesticate animals and grow their own food, when children learn that they can do things on their own and decide they no longer need their parent, here the ego is at its strongest point. Here the emotional pain of separation is fresh and experienced without defense. The pain itself becomes a barrier where once there was relationship. The ego takes control with a vengeance. Separation from caregiver, separation of the mind, is at its most intense and humanity is at its worst. Man learned to grow food, build homes and wage war upon their neighbors. To the victor went the spoils. Who so ever had the best weapons had the largest empire. To destroy one's enemy was a daily part of life. If the neighboring city-state was perceived as stronger than they were a threat, regardless of their intentions. The "other" must be destroyed in order that self could be preserved. The value of individual life was at its lowest point. Laws were strict and punishment harsh. It became important to identify yourself according to the status of others, social classes evolved as civilization did. Those on the lower end of the scale were of lesser value than those at the top. If someone had something more than you they were a threat to your sense of self. To enslave the "others" was perfectly acceptable. To kill, maim, desolate, sacrifice to the gods was a part of ancient life.

Within an individual life, this is middle school. Somewhere around the age of 11, children begin to question their identity. They begin their quest for self by comparing themselves to their peers. They arrange themselves in groups of like individuals. Their identity is determined by the company they keep. They are the athletes, geeks, Goths and the popular kids, and they all know their place in the strict social hierarchy. They don't really know who they are but they know who they are not. They know that the popular kids have the most value and the strange loner kids have none at all. They are vicious in their defense of self. They will degrade their peers yet have no understanding when it is done to them in return. They frequently use physical or emotional violence to assert themselves over others they feel have threatened their place in the social hierarchy. Their sense of self is utterly dependent on their status with regards to their peers, thus it is imperative that their peers not exceed them to any great degree. Violent incidents occur more frequently in middle school than at any other time. It is the reign of the ego and here the ego uses anger as a protection against pain. If you are verbally or physically beating up your classmate or slaughtering your neighbors you feel, at least for the moment, a tremendous sense of power. It appears as if you are in control, no one can question that. That is a very good thing for you because you cannot tolerate questions that might call into question your sense of reality. You are likely to be incapable of seeing beyond your own perception. Life is the way it is because that is how it should be. The gods, the priests or the King said it must be and the teacher, the school or your parents made the rules. You must follow the rules or the laws of order which have been given you. Rules or laws are necessary to maintain social order and may be exceedingly harsh but accepted as part of society. This does not mean that you like the way things are, you will likely be angry because after all you are simply a victim of fate. You have no true power over the events of your life.

Life is a quest for self. What defines the ages of man is the way in which humanity as a whole tends to answer the question, "who am I?" In this first age of the ego, characterized by anger, the question is answered for you by society. In the earliest civilizations and up to and beyond the Scientific Revolution, your identity was given to you at birth. There was no need to question, your life was pre-determined by your station, just as a teens life is still truly determined by their parents (which you may have noticed if you have one, makes them angry) You followed the rules as given to you by your master, your King or your God or your mother and father. You answer the question who am I by saying, I am who my people say I am. My status is dependent upon my position within the relative hierarchy, my status depends on others. In order for me to gain, others must lose. Anger is my most dominant emotion; I am a victim, at the mercy of the Gods or of fate. My actions have little to do with my success or failure.

Rebels in this time period were few and far between. They could be found however, those who had grown far beyond this age of man, those who recognized the ego's prison and tried to show others the way to Truth. They are our greatest spiritual teachers, whose message has been misunderstood far more than it has been understood.

As we grow, our thinking shifts, we become discontent with the answers given to us by others. Are we truly what other people tell us we are? That answer becomes increasingly uncomfortable, a coat that no longer fits. We begin to look for answers in another place. Still we look outside of ourselves, yet we seek to find a more comfortable coat. As the middle ages draw to a close a few brave souls begin to look at things in a new way. They observe the heavens and apply logic and reasoning to their observations. They determine that the earth is in fact not the center of the universe, the Church has been mistaken. It was a significant shift in our relative position in the universe, and a metaphor for the shift in thought. The Church is no longer without flaw, a fact they will go to great and violent lengths to conceal. If the Church can be mistaken, there must be another way to find answers. The Scientific method is born and will begin its quest to supersede faith with reason. It is now acceptable to question. The question will begin to be answered differently.

Now, the answer to the question, "who am I" becomes "I am the set of beliefs I choose to hold." The significant shift here is in the choice. As the middle ages end, serfs become free. The idea of freedom, of personal choice, or liberty begins to work its way into human consciousness. The French Declaration of the Rights of Man and the United States Declaration of Independence serve to articulate these ideas. The United States becomes an idea seeking its fruition. That the country will fall far short of their lofty goals of equality for man is less important than the setting of the goal itself. This is the time period in the individual life when adulthood has been reached. Society says at this time that you must make your own decisions and take responsibility for your own life. The question has the same answer… "I am the set of ideas I choose to attach myself to" As a free thinking adult I am a Liberal or a Conservative. I am Catholic or Protestant or atheist. I find a niche in my society or I define myself as outside of society, either way identity is tied to the ideas we hold. That we most often choose the identity given to us by our caregivers is ignored by many. We do not see that our identity has been chosen for us, we believe we have made the choice ourselves. Thus so has everyone else. We become frightened of those that hold alternate beliefs. If I am a Liberal than my ideas about society are correct. If a conservative were to be correct that would be a threat to my identity. The world controlled by the ego's fear is black and white. You must be one or the "other" and if you are the other, you are the enemy. This type of thinking tends to govern early adulthood. I like you because you are like me, I do not like you because you are not. I enjoy indulging in righteous anger. I am clearly correct and the fact that you cannot see that justifies my anger. This anger is more clearly rooted in fear than the blind unreasoning anger and judgment of the previous age.

The nature of law begins to change. A court system evolves allowing for testimony and an opportunity to defend oneself against accusation. Initially it is largely governed by the bias of the ruling class but as time goes on it evolves into an institution seeking to bring reason to judgment.

Wars in this time period are about ideology and identity. As Catholicism loses its control over Europe, there is much loss of life. Protestants and Catholics alike are willing to fight to the death to protect their beliefs. Religious freedom is a threat. Conflict over religion will continue for hundreds of years, even in the country founded on the basis of religious freedom. The Age of Imperialism combines elements of the previous age, in its desire to conquer for the sake of acquisition yet ideology plays a large part as well. As European countries used their superior military technology to dominate the rest of the Western Hemisphere they did not simply conquer and exploit their subjects, they insisted on trying to make them adopt European ideology. Missionaries went to spread the Gospels, school were built to teach English, they were taught that modern technology was superior to their traditional lifestyle. The European way was the only acceptable way. World War I was fought directly over national ideologies, or nationalism. The belief that to be German is better than to be French, or to be English far superior to Russian. Millions died to protect an ideological identity. World War II took the protection of ideology to its most extreme. Adolf Hitler played upon the Germans' diminished national identity. He told them that it had to be the "others' " fault that there country had suffered a humiliating defeat in World War I. The German ideology could not be wrong, there must be traitors among us and they are anyone who is not us. Their targets were anyone who stood out as not being a "good" German, The Jewish people, Gypsies, homosexuals…all those who might hold ideas that did not match Hitler's version of German society. To protect ourselves, he said, we must destroy them. This is the age of Social Darwinism, when intellect says that humans are of differing value based on their ability to reason in the "correct" way.

This is the world of the twenty- something. I know who I am because I know what I believe. I know that my ideas are superior to others. For most people in this age bracket, the strict hierarchy of middle school and high school socialization has passed. Though they may still occupy a social class it is not as relevant to their identity. No longer does society tell me who I am. I am certain my personal beliefs are who I am. For others to hold alternate beliefs is a threat to my being. If they are right, I am wrong. I must defend my beliefs in order to defend myself. This is a frightening place to occupy. Who I am is my choice…what if I choose incorrectly? This is a possibility too frightening to consider. I must choose between faith and reason. I must choose between right and wrong. I will define myself as good or bad. If I make the wrong decisions I will fail, I will be judged harshly by others and more importantly by myself. I am afraid that I may choose incorrectly. I am afraid of myself.

As we move into middle age we become more comfortable with ourselves. Our judgments of others tend to soften. We settle into a way of being that suits us, we wear a more comfortable coat. We have created a family or a career, or both. We may struggle to balance them but the more we have learned about ourselves the better able we are to create a satisfactory life. We are less quick to anger, more likely to have compassion. We are comfortable enough to engage in self-reflection, if we have not done so already. We recognize that the world does not revolve around us; the ego's hold begins to slip. It becomes increasingly difficult to blame others for our mistakes. A lifetime of evidence seems to prove that this is not so. Having children may encourage us to question some of the assumptions we have long held about our own childhood. We may be forced to look at things in a different way. Alternately, not having children may force us to do the same thing. There will be more time available for self-reflection. We are less willing to accept the ideas given to us by others. The values our parents taught us may simply not hold up to the lessons of our experiences.

This is an age where we begin to be willing to embrace Truth. We find that it is held in the balance, it is Buddha's middle way of compassion. Truth can never be found in opposing forces, it does not lie in the ego's judgment. I believe we are leaving the age of fear at this time in our collective existence. As human beings we are more likely to accept Truth than ever before in our past. We are closer to the ideal that all people are created equal. We no longer find it so readily acceptable for one country to invade and subjugate another, though it does still happen.

We no longer tolerate State-sanctioned slavery. Women in many countries are protected as equals with men. The United States ignored its Truth well past the Civil War. Not until the 1950s and the civil rights movement were we no longer allowed to rest comfortably in falsehood. It was a wakeup call. There is ultimate Truth; it does not lie in differing ideology. As a country and as individuals it began a significant shift.

For centuries humanity has told itself that feelings were not important, what was important was to keep them in check. Women especially bore the brunt of this stigma. To be emotional was to be weak. From the '50s on the number of people seeking psychiatric care or some type of counseling has steadily increased. We recognize now that one cannot bury emotions and expect them to go away. We have a far greater understanding of the role of the subconscious and the effect of buried emotions. It is now far more socially acceptable to talk about one's feelings. We have begun to embrace Truth though we are still limited by perception.

How then will we answer the question in this new age? Who am I? I may not be certain who I am, but I am not what others tell me. I am not a social class; I am not a set of ideas governed by perception. Quite possible I am a far different being than I have been taught to believe. I am not my body. I can see through perception if I am willing to embrace Truth. I can experience Peace. I can begin to understand that there is nothing I am not. There are no "others", no differences among us. We are all the same, there is no true conflict. There is a higher power and it is Love.

This is the age of Peace. It is a point at which the ego has lost its control. It may yet speak but we have learned to ignore it. Our focus has been placed on Love and on connection. We can now experience the passive energy of Love; we can give love to others with lessening reserve. This age, I think, will be shorter than that which came before it. It can lead to only one place, Joy, The full acceptance of Love and of ourselves. Here we will know ourselves complete. We will be one with the universal consciousness, we will be one as man and we shall choose our focus well.

These are broad and vast generalizations. Any historian worth their salt could point out any number of aberrations from my model, not to mention criticizing it for including only Western history. Yet, I believe there is great truth here. At any particular age there is a tendency for thinking to be predominately of one kind. Just as individuals do not mature at the same rate within a generation, the same is true in history. Though one group of people may advance to great achievements, others lag behind. I have met many people in my life who, as adults, are still locked in anger. They do not recognize its source; just accept that it is a natural part of themselves. They see it as normal to continually lash out at others. They may continue this way until they die of old age. It is the same historically as it is individually. Some will recognize and accept Truth faster and easier than others.

In every age there will be those who lag behind and those who charge ahead. Within each age you will find the balance tipping towards those who achieve a matching level of spiritual growth. As we grow, the ages become shorter, as the energetic pull of our oneness moves us to greater understanding. We have reached a point in our evolution where peace is possible. However, in many lives there is a midlife crisis. A point reached where one who has followed the dictates of society without self-questioning realizes that something has gone awry. What they believe was promised them for following the rules has not materialized. They are not happy. They have an identity that has no relationship to who they are. We may, as a people, face a midlife crisis. We may find that some of our kinds have reached a state of being that is frightening to those who have not. They will do, as humans dominated by their ego have always done, they will seek to eliminate what threatens them. Let us hope that this crisis is *not* a necessary step to our total acceptance of God's love.

Chapter 13

PERSONAL TRUTH

We all want to be loved. We accept this as a part of human nature. We do not want to feel pain. We accept this as well. Children, at least for a short time, expect only love. When they are inevitably disappointed, they feel painfully rejected. Yet they are told to stop crying, to be a big boy or girl. They are told in one way or another that their feelings are unacceptable. Many times this message comes from the ones who have caused the pain in the first place. They learn to hide their feelings. They learn so well that they are even able to hide feelings from themselves. Emotional injury is locked away for safe keeping, carefully stored so as not to be fully experienced. The more pain kept in the subconscious the greater the block to True Spirit and the greater hold the ego will have on focus.

This pain may remain with you your entire life. You may not even know it is there. You can have no idea why it is that some things make you angry. No idea why other things make you cry. It may never occur to you that in your attempt to spare yourself from pain, you created a way to hold onto it forever. The ego is most effective in keeping this system in place. In fact, the ego is dependent upon it. If you wish to escape its prison, you will have to look at truth. So long as you hold false ideas about yourself, you cannot see ultimate Truth. You cannot accept God's Love if you believe you are a being who should carry the heavy burden of stored pain. Every spiritual journey begins and ends with truth.

I use the term personal truth because it is what you believe about yourself. Your particular set of falsehoods. If you do not live your own truth, you cannot find spiritual Truth. Part of this truth is recognizing the ego for what it is. If you are willing to engage in self-reflection, and you cannot grow without doing so, you will have to acknowledge that many of the things you "think" do not make sense. You will be forced to acknowledge that you do not always understand your feelings. You do not always know why you do the things you do. This is an illogical state of being. It does not make sense that you do not know yourself.

Perhaps you have had an experience where you saw something of great beauty, so beautiful that it brought tears to your eyes. You tell yourself they are tears of joy for this marvelous sight. This is a lie. These are not tears of joy, what you feel is sorrow. You believe deep in your heart that you are not deserving of this beauty that something so extraordinary is outside of you and you will never experience the joy of its being. These are not the words that you will hear in your mind, but it is the pain you will feel in your heart. You must learn to listen to your heart and ignore the chatter in your head. Your personal truth lies in your heart and not in your head.

Only when you have stilled the chatter and sit in quiet contemplation are the words in your head likely to reflect truth.

You will need to admit to yourself that there is a part of you that does not want to be happy. For some this is a large part, others smaller and perhaps for the fortunate few, nonexistent. This is the part of you that watches sad movies when you are sad, or drags out the old photographs of the one who has left you. It is important not to bury emotions, they must be experienced, but we do not need to work at making our selves feel worse. This is the part of you that tells you negative things about yourself. It says that you are stupid or unattractive or that people do not like you. What would be the point of this except to make you unhappy? Self-reflection does not require self-debasement, it does however require honesty. When you see that you have made mistakes in the past, learn from them and let them go. Realize that you did the best that you could at that time. If you chose to belittle yourself for your shortcomings you are allowing the ego to tell you who you are. The ego does not know truth, it can never know you.

As you begin to disengage your emotions from your ego you will find more space to grow. You may begin to recognize that some of your reactions to other human beings in the past have been decidedly unfair. You allowed your particular brand of perception to mete out what saw as just punishment for whatever their offense. You may still be engaged in this type of emotional response.

Take a moment to consider the people in your life with whom you have the most interaction. It is likely that they sometimes make you angry. In fact, it is likely that if you think just for a moment about whatever it is that makes you the angriest, you will begin to feel angry with them right now. As you sit here and read these words they may be thousands of miles away but you are still angry. So now I ask you to consider, who is making you angry? Why are you willing to become angry about something that is not even occurring at this time? The truth is that you want to be angry, or at least a part of you does. If you spend a great deal of time thinking angry thoughts you are allowing the ego to reign unchecked over your being. You may tell yourself that you cannot help being angry. You may tell yourself you can't control your own thoughts. If you do not control your thoughts, then who does? Is it the person who makes you angry? Can their actions or words really control you? Whose mind generates your thoughts? Are you really controlled by someone else?

There have undoubtedly been times in your life when someone wanted you to feel a certain way about something. They may have done everything in their power to convince you to do so. You could not however be persuaded to agree. In this case, did they control your emotions? Clearly here they did not. Yet sometimes, when it is convenient for you, you may say that they do. Do you sometimes abdicate your thoughts to others? Is it, by chance, when you have particularly negative thoughts that you attribute their source to others? Does that make sense? No, it does not, and in fact you do not make sense. The you that believes it is ego does not make sense. We think anger gives us strength, we think fear protects us from harm; we think preferences are who we are. We think there are times when compassion is unwarranted.

Yet you must understand, it is your choice to allow the ego to define you and it is your choice to say it may no longer do so.

The people in your life who cause you the most distress have the most important lessons to teach you about yourself. They are in your life for a reason; you chose to allow them to be a part of it because you know they are like you. Consider the characteristic you find most irritating about other human beings. If you are willing to look deeply within yourself you will find that it is the characteristic you like least about yourself. That which you find most difficult to forgive in others is what you cannot forgive in yourself. You may deny this, likely you will, but the emotion is in you, not in them. For me, it was arrogance. One human being behaving as if they were superior to another really got under my skin. It took a very long time for me to understand that this was my problem and not theirs. I came to understand that I wanted to be better than other people; I truly wanted to be special. I thought that that was how one acquired value, yet I would not allow myself to believe that I was of great value. I was like them. I did not express it in the same way but at my core I felt it. This was a lesson slowly learned. We do not want to admit that all of our negative feelings reside within ourselves. They are what we believe to be true about our self.

In this plane of human existence it is not possible for us to perfectly meet the needs of another human being. In truth we are not meant to. No other human being can ever make us happy; we should not expect them to. When you place this expectation on another you create an impossible situation. They can never be what you want because what you want is to feel completely loved. It is you who must accept the love that is within you. Until you do so, other human beings can act only as a mirror, giving back to you only what you are willing to accept. They may love you deeply but if love does not reside in your heart you will be unable to accept it. You will find reason to deny it; you will find reason to be angry. You will judge others as you judge yourself and you will not know love.

Consider for a moment what it might be like to feel whole, utterly complete, loved and loving. Do you have the need to judge anyone? Think back to a time when you were first falling in love. Were you more or less judgmental? Weren't you better able at this time to overlook things that you might not ordinarily have overlooked? Then consider a time when you may have broken up or lost a loved one, how did this impact your view of others? When you are personally suffering is this not the time that you judge others most harshly? When you feel great about yourself it is much easier to accept others. Spend some time in stillness considering this. Whatever you do, do not choose to criticize yourself; you might as well shoot yourself in the foot. Criticizing yourself for being critical of others will only make you feel worse and thus make you more critical. The goal is for you to see Truth, so that you may know yourself above question or criticism.

You will come to a point where you will recognize all judgment as originating with your feelings about self. If you are comfortable with your place in this world you will find far less to judge than if you are not. Most of us believe that judgment is intrinsic in human nature, something we cannot escape. It is in judgment that you find pain. If you accepted all events without judgment there would be no loss. If you are upset because you are losing your house, your pain does not reside with the house. What you are truly upset about is how losing the house is going to make you feel. If you believe there is a difference between living in a mansion and living in a homeless shelter, the difference is solely in the way you feel about it. The greater our degree of preference, the more we judge, the less acceptance we have of self.

You must learn to be honest with yourself. You may think this is a simple matter but you have been in the habit of deceiving yourself since your ego developed the ability to speak. You do not want to feel pain and so you tell yourself it is not there. You must be perfectly honest with yourself here, when love is absent you feel pain, you live in the absence of your true self. When a loved one becomes angry or upset with you and temporarily or perhaps permanently removes their love from you, this is a painful event. Many will use anger in this circumstance to deflect the pain. How dare they be angry with me for that? They have done the very same thing hundreds of times…they are being selfish….I had a right to do what I did…they are just being ridiculous…instead of, ouch that hurts. That is the truth of the situation. Withdrawal of love is painful, regardless of circumstances. It is never justified, yet it is inherently human. We do not believe in eternal Love, we believe in loss. Until we reach a higher state of consciousness where we are connected to Love's source we must do our best to be honest about the nature of human love. It is given and withdrawn at a dizzying rate. When it is withdrawn we have a tendency to revert to childish behavior in an effort to deflect the pain. Only if you are willing to recognize the truth will you be able to avoid self-destructive behavior that makes the situation worse. Admit to yourself that your co-worker's criticism stings, that your friend's rejection hurts, that divorce is painful, but do so without deflection. Do not try to pass the pain back to the person that you believe has given it to you. That will simply intensify the pain and loss. Try to remember that you are dealing with ego and perception, yours and theirs. You are not dealing with their True self. Any desire to harm another human being is rooted in ego. It is telling you the lie that to harm another human being will make you stronger, that to take something from them will make you the winner. Only the ego's judgment sees winners and losers. We are all the same; we all feel love's loss. Someone who is attacking you does so because they are themselves experiencing loss. They are feeling diminished and listening to their ego telling them how to make it better. If you intensify their pain, you do the same to your own, no matter what lie you tell yourself.

Spiritual growth requires a willingness to see truth where you would prefer to believe lies. You must be willing to accept responsibility for your circumstances. When you blame someone or something else you deny yourself the chance to grow. This may be the most difficult thing to accept on our path. When you suffer it is because you have chosen to suffer. When you experience physical pain or illness, you do so because you have made this choice. You have not made the decision consciously, for were you fully conscious you would have no need of such experiences. You made this choice because in whatever circumstances you find yourself, this is your best chance to grow. You have been unable to learn your next lesson in an easier way and so you have hit a road block. The pain or illness will continue until you are able to clear the blockage. It may come and go, if so, pay close attention to the circumstances in your life when it is active. We have all been sick, we have all been injured, we all believe we should suffer. We judge ourselves the harshest of all. Do not then make the mistake of placing self-judgment on others. If you find yourself disdainful of those who are continually ill, then know that you cannot stand the weakness that you perceive to be in yourself. As we extend compassion to others, we must first accept it for ourselves.

The deeper our willingness to understand personal truth, the greater our understanding of universal Truth. We must begin to see ourselves in a different light. We are not our circumstances; we are not the outcome of events. To say that I will be all right if things work out the way I want them to, is far different than to say that I am always all right. We do not know how events and outcomes will truly impact us. We cannot see the whole; the ego's perception is a narrow point of focus which no one else can share. Truth allows us to move beyond perception. To give up judgment is not to condone suffering, yet certainly to embrace compassion is to see suffering end.

For most of us, the journey to personal truth is a painful road. If you do not believe this is true you may want to look again. Many people live long lives hiding from what they believe to be true about themselves, ideas that no one else may share. It is likely that you have done such a good job at hiding from yourself that you have no idea where to start looking. If your words and your actions are not in alignment you are not living in truth. If you cause harm to yourself or others, you are not living in truth. If you have emotional responses that you do not understand this is the place to begin the search. If you reach a point in your journey where you begin to feel as if you understand more, you are seeing things differently, things that most other people cannot see and it makes you feel special, it is now time for the really hard work to begin.

In order to be special, you must be separate. To bare your soul is to see that what resides in your heart, resides in the heart of all. You have, stored within you, false ideas, mistruths you chose to believe were you. We will each come to the end of our journey one day and there we will find our self. It is unlikely that we will get there without having faced painful truths. When we find the courage to seek Truth through the pain, we will find it. Achieving lasting peace and joy is a matter of giving up what we are not. You are not the things that you do. You are not the roles that you play. You are not the things that you like or dislike. Nothing that is outside of you can possibly define who you are.

Part III

TRUE CONSCIOUSNESS

Chapter 14

TRUE CONSCIOUSNESS

Outside of time, we know ourselves. We are the originating consciousness, an indistinguishable dimension of the whole. To us was given all. In this womb of consciousness we grew, emerging awareness. We shared awareness with our father as we came to know that we were. Awareness grew, and awareness narrowed. We came to hold our own focus. We knew our self as one with our Father, we knew our self as one. We came to believe that to know our selves meant to deny God, to have self we must have separation. We shifted our focus from universal awareness to an individual point of self. In this imagined move away from God, we became lost. We lost our awareness of the energy of consciousness; we lost our connection to Love. In this chasm of darkness we fell. We did not understand that this was an imagined loss that nothing exists outside the mind of God. Instead we deemed ourselves cast out by our creator, judged unworthy of his Love. We, who had once known the universe entire, now could not even know our self. We experienced the absence of Love as crushing, shattering shame. What might have sent us back to our Father instead drove us further from him. We believed that this shame was his punishment for our betrayal. We believe we are unworthy of God's Love. We searched for relief from the pain that now occupied the core of our being. We allowed our focus to drift and found shelter in deception. We gave our self to the ego in exchange for its promise of protection. We have shaped our existence on its lies.

The time has come for us to return to Truth. We must see that there is no Truth in the ego's perceptions. It cannot truly see, it looks through the filter of its own imaginings to show you the world it has created. Here you are alone; here you will always be alone. The ego can never know truth; its existence is dependent on deception. In order for it to continue to be you must believe you are unworthy of God's Love. The ego can only tell you lies. It will convince you that what is most important is the past or the future, not the present moment. It will tell you that others are not like you and their differences are a threat to your identity. It tells abused children that they are responsible for the abuse. It tells the alcoholic whose life is spiraling out of control that having a drink will make things better. It tells the person struggling to lose weight that having something to eat will make them feel better. It tells you that the way to solve a problem is to demand your way and to be angry and resentful if you do not get it. It tells you that to not get your way is to lose something of yourself. It tells you that other people control your emotions. It insists that you see yourself through others judgmental eyes while denying that judgment can only come from within. It is happy to remind you of all your faults and flaws. It enjoys replaying painful memories especially when you begin to feel happy. The ego is not God's creation. Truth cannot know deception.

Focus is an aspect of awareness. It is the part of us that allows for choice. We have the power to choose where to place our focus, but we have forgotten that it is our choice. The ego has hijacked our focus and has no intention of giving it back. In Truth we experience that which we choose to experience. If we wish to turn our focus away from universal consciousness we may do so, but it is still held in our distant awareness. Even in our state of separation our mind is capable of holding multiples points of focus and awareness. As I sit at my computer, I focus on what I am writing, yet I am aware of the room I am sitting in, the little dog at my feet. As I shift my focus into broader awareness I recognize the hum of the computer and the sound of the crickets outside and I know that I have been vaguely aware of them all along. Such is the incredible power of our mind, even in its unnaturally diminished state. The ego must be a constant distraction to keep us from remembering from whence we came. It tells you stories about the past, stories about the future and stories about its imagined present. It applies multiple labels to everything it "sees." There, it says, is a flower. It is pink, it is pretty, it is not as pretty as the one I saw yesterday. I like that kind of flower. I wonder if I could buy that plant for my yard. It does everything in its considerable power to keep you from experiencing the flower. Our ability to create lies in our focus. The reason I have been able to write this book is that I am able to place my focus on understanding the things I wanted to understand. I am able to find enough stillness that allows my focus to settle on this one thing, at least for a period of time. Creative expression comes from your True self. It is inherent in your nature. It is the sculpture that exists within the stone, the song which is discovered rather than written, the story born before it was put to paper. Creation is your birthright. When you create you know yourself in that moment. You are no longer victim, you are master. To live without creation is to exist as a shadow of your true self. So long as the ego holds the entirety of your focus you forfeit your inheritance.

Most of us, at this time in our evolution, act and "think" from competing levels of consciousness, the ego, which is completely, and utterly unconscious, and the subconscious which may or may not be fully stocked with your personal untruths. We know that it holds at the very least, the idea that you are unworthy of God's Love. If it did not, or had not at some point in this lifetime, you would not be here. The sole purpose of our existence on this planet is to learn who we are so that we can exist in Truth. When we have done that, we no longer need this particular classroom. When our focus is narrow, held entirely by the ego, our lessons come slowly. They come one at a time and may be very difficult to master. One who believes themselves to be a finite dot has a difficult time accepting that they are the infinite whole.

In Truth the subconscious is our being, we are what we feel. All of our emotions are centered around love. They either reflect a shade of its presence or the specter of its absence. We can attach our identity to any number of titles or roles but these do not describe self, only the part we chose to play for a time. Our body is itself only a reflection of our emotional state of being. Whatever pain our subconscious holds will manifest itself in a corresponding system. The subconscious determines where we place our focus. Our level of awareness determines our focus. If our subconscious is full of pain, all we can know of our self is pain and thus our ego is allowed to control focus. As we clear false pain from our subconscious awareness the ego begins to lose its hold. Our focus can begin to see Truth. The shift away from ego allows our focus to gradually assume its true nature. It begins to break through the veil of perception. It may see the world as it is. It loses its need to judge, to measure, to label, it gives up on the notion of need altogether. It sees the world is as human beings have made it. It knows that in truth, there is only Love. It understands that when people are ready to shift their focus, the world will shift with them. Awareness holds knowledge that does not come through perception. Enlightenment, or expanded understanding, is a matter of shifting our focus to allow for expanded awareness. The awareness has always been there, only pushed far into the background.

We live in a time when people are far more willing to look at Truth. We recognize that buried emotions continue to guide our actions until we deal with them and let them go. We believe that Truth can be found in the rational and logical evaluation of reality. God does not require us to abdicate reason to know Truth, he does not hide. We are meant to see divinity in all things. Though we live in a world of our own making, isolated by perception, we have never been alone. We have always been held safely in God's awareness. He waits for us to understand that ultimate Truth exists in both science and faith. It does not matter which course you choose to follow, so long as you do not allow yourself to be misled by your own personal deceptions.

The manner in which we deceive ourselves is multilayered. At the core is the pain of rejection, our shared shame. We use fear most effectively as a barrier. If we are deeply within the ego's grip we also readily engage in anger to cover the fear. As we grow spiritually, as our focus shifts, fear moves from something outside of ourselves to something within us. We come to realize that this internal place has been the source of our fear all along. It is this that is hardest for us to let go. We are sure if we do, that we will be destroyed. In a sense we are afraid of our pain. We are afraid that God's Love will annihilate our being because we are unworthy of it. We are, in part, correct. The fear driven creature that you have been will cease to be. What is left will be what you have always been, a being of light and Love, one with no understanding of the ego's insanity. To stand at this crossroads, you will already have let go most of the things that were not truly you. Your ego may still exist but it will hold no sway over your emotional being. You will see your fellow human beings for what they are, you will have ceased to judge. You will know that all human actions are motivated by the desire to acquire Love and see that it is the ego that twists their attempts into self–destruction. Never has there been one among us, who shown the True nature of God's Love, would turn his back on it. In knowing this Love we finally know ourselves and the question, who I am, is finally answered. What you give up when you surrender this last shred of fear are the things that you have never been. You will step into a world which is only light. Here there is no shadow to block even an instant of Joy.

Peace passes through you in a gentle stream of shared consciousness. You hold on to nothing as you have no need to fill. You are the rhythm of the universe.

Every time your heart is broken there is a reason why. God is calling you to look through the pain, to see truth. He is there on the other side. Your refusal to deal honestly with pain locks you on the other side of love. He wants you to see that what you are afraid of is not him but yourself. You are afraid that you do not have the strength to face this pain of love's loss and so you look away. The more pain and heartache you survive, the stronger your belief in your ability to handle anything, the more firmly you live in truth. It you crumble and fall when love is lost you are living a lie. You must feel the pain, shed every last tear and see who you truly are. Know that in your heart is the love that fills the universe. Yours is a heart that can never break, a heart that could never withdraw love from another. This is what lies on the other side of the pain.

The ego tells us that to elevate ourselves to the status of God is to place ourselves in a position of superiority over others. It is certain that this is insanity. We could not possibly be one with our creator. It tells us we must occupy a place of diminished status. Our proper relationship with our creator is that of judge and judged. It tells us that our perfect Father created flawed beings. That one who is the origin of Love, withheld perfection from us and that when we do not live up to his expectations we deserve his punishment. It tells us that we might find salvation in following a strict set of rules. In order to believe this it must identify others who will not be saved because they do not follow the same rules. The ego tells us that to forgive is to condone injustice. To absolve Hitler and the Nazis is to make light of the death of millions of innocents. This is not so. Suffering in all its forms must be met with compassion. We must learn to show one another that if you are not acting out of Love, you are acting out of its absence. If you have chosen the role of conqueror or chosen the role of victim, you have placed yourself outside of Love.

Perfection has no need of judgment. Perfection knows no lack, it knows itself whole and complete, it does not need to see imperfection in others to know itself thus. As completion it knows all as self, it shares self with all of its creation. Love withholds nothing, it asks only that you learn to do the same.

At an emotional level, we believe that to be one with our father is to cease to be. That if we allow ourselves to be God, there is no longer self. Our ego is certain this is an impossible scenario. It is certain we must maintain a separate identity in order to exist. To exist and be of value we must be special in some way, different and distinct from others. The ego itself does not exist, it is not a part of consciousness, it is an aspect of distorted focus. Its world is imagined and imagined out of fear. At the heart of the ego is always untruth. It tells you it can make you happy and yet in true happiness is its undoing. It must make you unhappy, miserable if it can, in order to "know" itself safe. Truth is its enemy. The ego is sure that love is pain, it always involves loss. This is the ego's truth. You must move past ego to see Truth.

Our world believes in loss. When tragedy strikes we question God. How could he do this to innocent people, or somewhat more charitably, how could he allow this to happen? Would a loving god allow earthquakes, tsunamis, tornadoes and hurricanes? Would he allow children to suffer from cancer? Your father would not have you suffer even an instant of discomfort. He would allow your consciousness to grow without the pain of separation. It is we who would not allow this. We embraced the belief that separation was possible; choosing to believe that there could be loss and substituted this for our Father's Love. It is our choices to learn through pain.

You cannot deny that is is the most difficult times in our lives that make us stronger. When we lose our home and all of our possessions, we come to a spiritual crossroads. We must either accept that we are not our possessions or be destroyed along with them. As we rebuild we see that that what we thought was lost forever can be replaced. It is the feeling of safety and security that returns with time. Disaster provides for us the opportunity to allow others to help us. This is a gift given to both in equal measure. Your willingness to accept allows them to truly give. There is great Truth in this. Tragedy will show you strength that you did not know was there and it will show you the tremendous capacity for Love human beings have for one another. You may curse God for what he has taken from you, but this is a chance for you to lose mistaken ideas. You are not your home, your possessions or even your family. What is real cannot be lost.

It is understandable human nature to grieve the loss of a loved one. You know their loss only through perception. You can no longer see them, or hear them; your arms can no longer hold them. The senses are a highly faulty means of interpreting reality. They cannot know Truth. In a quiet moment, if grief can for a moment step aside, you may feel the presence of your loved one. In escaping the bonds of the body they have also escaped the filter of perception. Perhaps there is some comfort in knowing that though you perceive and grieve their loss, they do not grieve for the loss of you. Now their awareness is free and intimately connected with yours. You feel you have lost them; they know they will never lose you.

The body you lay to rest was only a temporary home. Your loved one cannot be lost, they are with you always in awareness. Love cannot be separated. Truth cannot be made false. When you are ready to look away from the ego, ready to look deeply inside yourself for your own truth, you will experience deepening awareness which will include everything and everyone. You cannot lose those you love, Love cannot be lost.

You are not alone in these lessons; there is a gentle guiding force at work. It sends rainbows and butterflies and dogs like you had when you were a kid: whatever message of comfort you are willing to accept. That which you need to grow is always given to you, even if it is simple reassurance. You must only be willing to see it. The ego will not see these things or will make of them something they are not.

We are meant to see divinity in all things. Our earth and all of our experiences are meant to show us Truth. Our perception shows us opposites, our awareness knows only balance. We struggle here because we insist on living on one side or the other. All life here is metaphor for Truth. Even time is a metaphor for separation. We have taken the continuity of being and segmented it into past and future. We can never know the present moment, where there is only Truth, so long as the ego holds sway. This moment will always be measured according to the past or by its value to the future. In quiet stillness is all that is. What we seek for is always here, hiding in plain sight. The only limit on your ability to see is your willingness to let go of what you are not. You must let go of anger and free the past, you must let go of fear and free the future. To believe that history is a metaphor for the evolution of consciousness, is to acknowledge only that we humans tend to take the more difficult path. We hold on to false ideas thinking they will keep us safe. Eventually we will all know that what is false is not true and we will be free. This is the difference between living in Truth and living a lie.

A lie is a heavy burden to carry and we have become all too accustomed to dishonesty. We lie to ourselves on a daily basis. We tell ourselves we are fine when we are not. We work ourselves to the point of exhaustion and say that is how it must be. We do not work at all and tell ourselves there is no other choice. We justify actions we know will cause harm. We take pills, and drink, and eat to cover pain rather than acknowledge and deal with it. We torment ourselves, each other, our world, all in a desperate bid to avoid that which we believe is our deepest personal truth, that we are unworthy of love. We all want the same thing, we want to feel Love. When we do not feel this way, we experience a painful existence. Stop running from pain, it runs right along with you.

To be afraid of yourself is insanity. How can you ever know a moment's rest when you believe there are aspects of yourself from which you must hide? You have created an elaborate charade and you labor heavily under its burden, every moment a struggle you do not recognize, to keep it intact. You do not see how tired you have become, pretending to be something you are not. You seek rest but have forgotten where to find it. You think the sleep of those who are already dreaming will provide for you what you need.

Fear is the belief that you do not now, or will not at some point in the future, have what you need to be alright. It is essentially self-doubt. You believe that the loss of possession or of a particular situation can leave you vulnerable. It is your lack of faith in yourself that is the issue. If you knew that nothing of real value could ever be lost, you would never be afraid. What you fear is the imagined condition of your being. It is not the tragic event; it is the way you think it will make you feel. You believe that you have lost something of yourself, that you are now somehow less than you were before.

You think your identity lies in separation, to be of value you must be unique. If you are not special in some way your existence has no meaning. You believe that to give up preference means to give up identity. You believe that to share every aspect of yourself means that you will no longer be. These are mistakes born in shame.

We are one energy system and we have chosen a difficult path. We are not judged for our choice, it was ours to make. That we struggle, fight and suffer is our chosen method of advancement, but it makes the going slow. There is only one possible outcome. We will be what we are. You believe this means the end of your awareness, that by sharing yourself entirely you will be lost in the vastness of consciousness. What you give up is anger, fear, and pain. What you gain is the universe entire.

Let go of the pain you hold as a barrier to your true self. Let go of the pain you have stored in this life, in past lives, in all of your human experience. Let go of the idea that you are unworthy of God's Love. You are God's Love, you always have been, you have simply forgotten that this is so. Find Joy in this knowledge, there is no pain here. Do not weep at what you feel is undeserved. God does not weep with you, he does not share your pain. He knows you as perfection only. He waits for you to return home when you are ready. Your true self is held always in his awareness. There is no lie the ego can tell to change this. You are safe, you have always been safe, you are God's Love.

We do not understand the true nature of love. We believe it is a give and take. We require that others love us, but in looking for love outside of ourselves we distort its true nature. If we give love we are by definition diminished in the giving. If we receive love from another we take something in return. In a truly loving relationship a balance may be struck here but still love is seen as an external entity. We are a people that believe in loss. We believe that love is in limited supply rather than the totality of experience. We do not know that we are one in shared awareness. To give and receive requires two separate entities, it is a dualistic concept. There is only Love and it seeks to give of itself. We are one energy field that extends itself through Love. Love is like breath, it holds a gentle rhythm. You breathe in and out, one action is inherent in the other until the day your body dies. You cannot hold your breath and expect it to sustain you. You cannot empty your lungs without refilling them. It is the gentle rhythm of the universe. To attempt to hold on to Love is to try and separate it from its source. Love is the flow of being, there is no division. It is within you, it is outside of you, it is all things. Opening yourself to Love benefits all, there can be no loss. When you acknowledge or allow the love inside you to be what it is, the sum total of self, it is naturally and without thought, given to everyone. The giving brings only increase. We think we hold on to things because we don't have enough when in fact it is the very act of holding on that keeps us from receiving more. We hold ourselves separate from the abundance of the universe. It is allowing yourself to receive that allows the energy of creation to flow through you and the peace and joy of God to settle upon you.

We hold three dimensions of consciousness. We are universal consciousness, we are human consciousness and we hold our own focus. So long as we choose to focus on untruth, to believe the lies we tell ourselves, we cut ourselves off from the shared awareness of humanity and the all-encompassing Love of our Father. In Truth these dimensions are seamless, they are one, there is no division. Love does not withhold. If you truly believed in your heart that there was no part of you that must be kept hidden from others you would live in this Truth. If you believed every ounce of your soul was good, you would withhold nothing. In our human consciousness we have stored a lie. It is a false thought that has become a barrier between our self and God. Here you believe that focus is the ego and awareness is emotion. You believe that you have become a separate entity and that in so doing you took something from your creator. You have branded yourself a thief and imposed the harshest possible penalty, life as we know it. What you did not understand was that this was not a choice that could ever be made.

To live in a state of separation from God is to place artificial divisions between levels of mind. Mind is all that we are. This is how we have become lost in our own consciousness. So long as we place fear and pain between ourselves and God we cannot go home. We believe that love is pain, thus we have entered a world that supports our beliefs. We see through the mirror of a fractured mind. We are drops of water who have forgotten they are the ocean. We believe that to be ocean means the end of our existence.

We spend our lives working our way back to our original mistake. To give up the notion that to be one with God is to lose self and to remove shame from our shared psyche. We have piled layer upon layer of falsehood to cover it. We are a people that have preferred denial to Truth. Beneath the shame is the original separating thought, "I cannot be both an individual and equally a part of the whole. It is not possible to be a distinct entity with my own focus and yet be in a state of eternal connection with all that is. It was simply a natural part of our evolution, that we went from universal awareness, to awareness of self-learning to find our own balance, to the ability to direct our consciousness in a particular focus. This is growth; nothing stunts growth more than shame. You have thoughts which originate in your focus, this is creation, but these thoughts are shared with all. Without shame there is no division. We are an idea given full expression, an idea given unto itself. You can allow your focus to settle on ego and know fear, you can allow your focus to settle on the subconscious and know pain, you can place your focus on spirit and know self. If you focus on hate, you will live in a world of hate, if you focus on Love, then that is where you will live. You can be as a drop without denying that you are ocean.

We must let go of all the ideas we have acquired about who we are and all of the judgments we have levied against ourselves and others. We allow this understanding through acceptance. So long as we judge we limit the scope of our understanding. We place large portions of the world outside of ourselves and say to ourselves I am not that. What you are rejecting is in fact the core of your being. To accept self is to accept all. Here there is no judgment, not of past, present or future. No longer is the state of self, dependent on outcome. In relinquishing outcome we reject fear entirely. It does not matter what happens because whatever it is we know we can handle it. Our emotional state of being is no longer controlled by the external world. Whatever your path to self holds is accepted. It need not hold wealth, or power or even the people we think we would chose to come along. It is a path we travel alone, yet at its end is everything and everyone. If we can narrow our focus to the True point of self, all that is will come into awareness.

There are no wrong turns, no points in your journey from which you cannot recover. Even if you have been traveling down a long bitter and barren road, it is always within your power to turn around. You may move slowly or quickly as is your choice. Some people may choose to come with you and some will choose to stay behind. They will make their choice another day. Do not think that choosing to remain with them will hasten their decision. We all move at our own speed in our own time. How different would our world be if we all believed that there was no mistake we could ever make that would separate us from our Father? If you held tightly to this knowing, would you feel fear? Would there be any reason to attack another human being? Consider that what has changed your life is an idea, a thought you chose to hold above all others.

Every person that walks into a church, temple, mosque or other place of worship with a quiet longing in their heart is looking for Truth. They seek to know God and through him their selves. They believe they will find peace in this knowledge and they are correct. Scientists and theologians ask the same question, they look for the same answer. Who are we and where can we find Truth? God took a piece of himself and gave it unto itself, withholding nothing. He gave it his own awareness; he gave it its own focus. He did this because it is his nature. Love seeks to give of itself, knowing that in the giving there is increase for all. Anyone who embraces Love as the center of their faith has found Truth.

When we know ourselves complete our heart and mind are one, all fear and anger are gone. Past and future merge into the present moment. Divisions evaporate, you no longer hold yourself separate. There is no preference, no judgment, no desire, no need or want, you are finally whole, as you now realize you have always been. You have turned your focus away from self-defeating fear, away from deprivation to Truth, the only place you could ever find yourself. It is only because you do not know yourself that you hang on to pain as if it were you. In your hands you hold the power of creation. You are Love, in Joy will you create, in peace will you rest. You will hold your own focus, it is yours to place as you will, but never would you deny it to others who might wish to share it with you. You do not withhold your experience under the banner of individuality. You do not need separation to know yourself. You will be connected in awareness always, so that you may relax your focus and rest, rest truly in the arms of your creator and know his peace, so that you may wake in Joy and know creation. You may be as a drop or be as the ocean.

Our world is a beautiful symphony, every note in its proper place, every crescendo, every pause. If you have been playing a different tune than the rest that is just fine. If at times notes clash and pauses are not always in unison that is also fine, everything is always as it should be. One day you will hear the tune that has always been. It is held deeply in your awareness and it waits only for you to find it.

It is a love song that calls us home. It carries the perfect pitch, at the perfect tempo, played for you alone. It stirs gentle memories. It is carried on a warm ocean breeze. It whispers all is well. It sings to you that suffering is not possible and smiles with you as you see this is so. It is a song like no other. It tells you that to believe you could suffer is insanity and that it is time to wake up. God waits patiently for you, judging nothing you think you have ever done, until the moment you are willing to step out of time and be one with eternity.